LEGO NINJAGO™

Masters of Spinjitzu

RISE OF THE SERPENTINE

LEGO® GRAPHIC NOVELS AVAILABLE FROM TITAN™

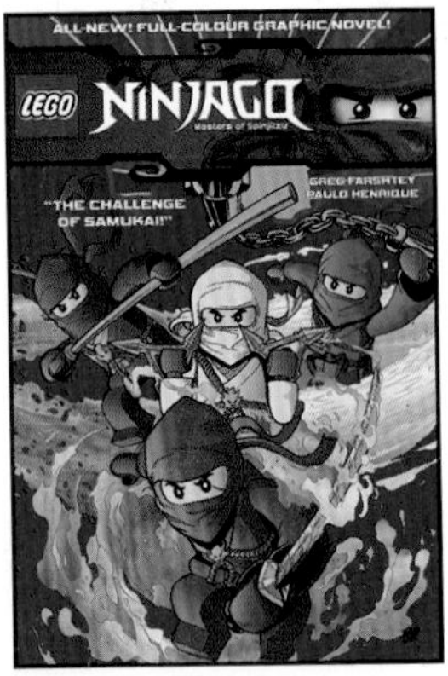
ALL-NEW! FULL-COLOUR GRAPHIC NOVEL!
LEGO NINJAGO
"THE CHALLENGE OF SAMUKAI!"
GREG FARSHTEY PAULO HENRIQUE
NINJAGO #1 (on sale now)

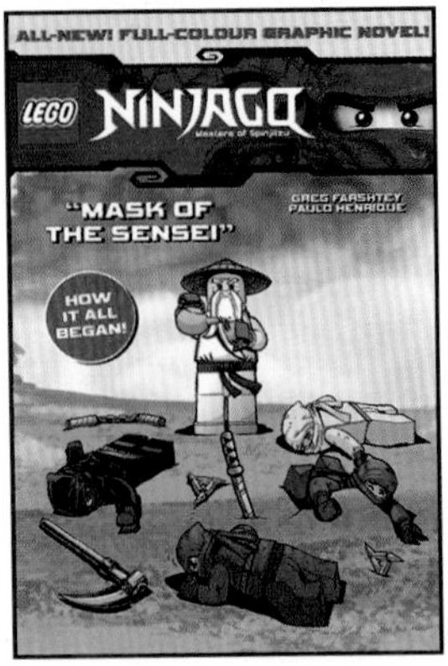
ALL-NEW! FULL-COLOUR GRAPHIC NOVEL!
LEGO NINJAGO
"MASK OF THE SENSEI"
GREG FARSHTEY PAULO HENRIQUE
HOW IT ALL BEGAN!
NINJAGO #2 (on sale now)

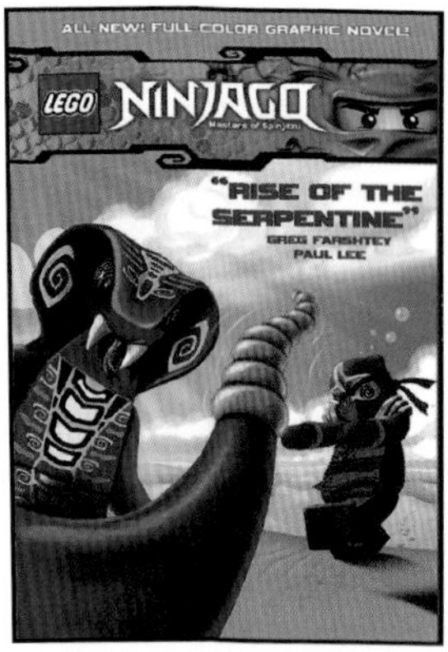
ALL-NEW! FULL-COLOR GRAPHIC NOVEL!
LEGO NINJAGO
"RISE OF THE SERPENTINE"
GREG FARSHTEY PAUL LEE
NINJAGO #3 (7 Nov 14)

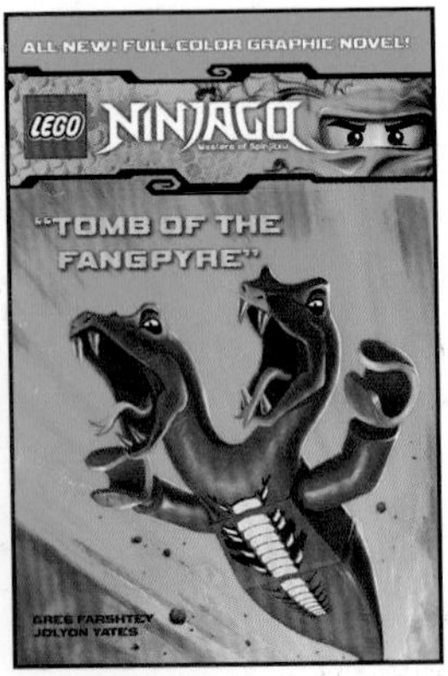
ALL-NEW! FULL-COLOR GRAPHIC NOVEL!
LEGO NINJAGO
"TOMB OF THE FANGPYRE"
GREG FARSHTEY JOLYON YATES
NINJAGO #4 (7 Nov 14)

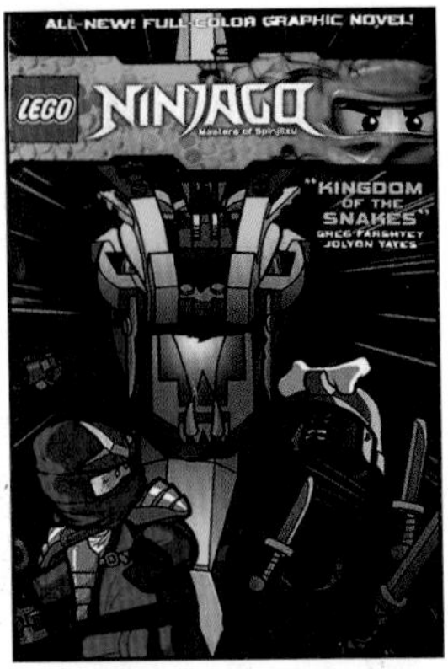
ALL-NEW! FULL-COLOR GRAPHIC NOVEL!
LEGO NINJAGO
"KINGDOM OF THE SNAKES"
GREG FARSHTEY JOLYON YATES
NINJAGO #5 (5 Dec 14)

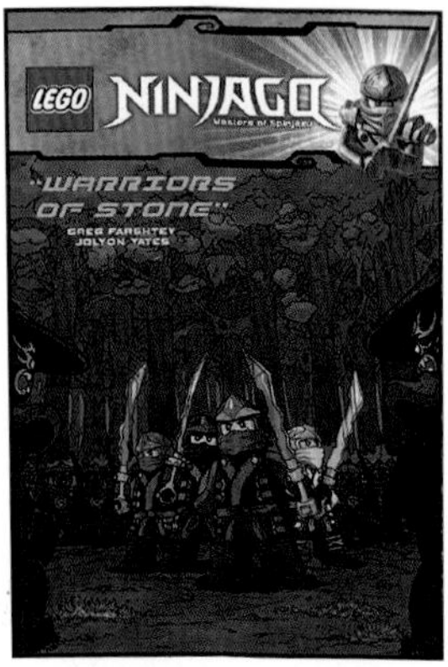
LEGO NINJAGO
"WARRIORS OF STONE"
GREG FARSHTEY JOLYON YATES
NINJAGO #6 (5 Dec 14)

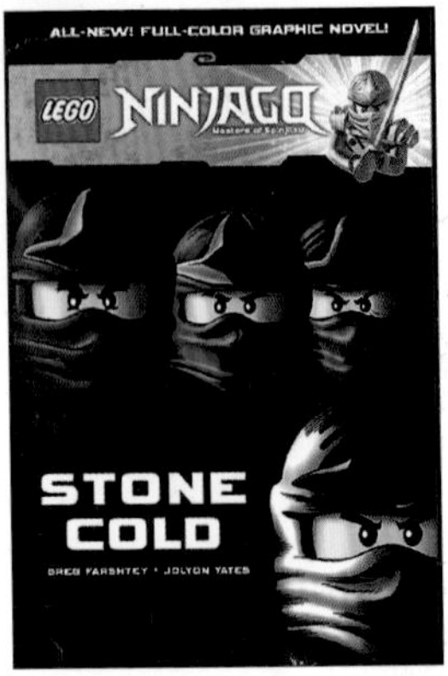
ALL-NEW! FULL-COLOR GRAPHIC NOVEL!
LEGO NINJAGO
STONE COLD
GREG FARSHTEY • JOLYON YATES
NINJAGO #7 (2 Jan 15)

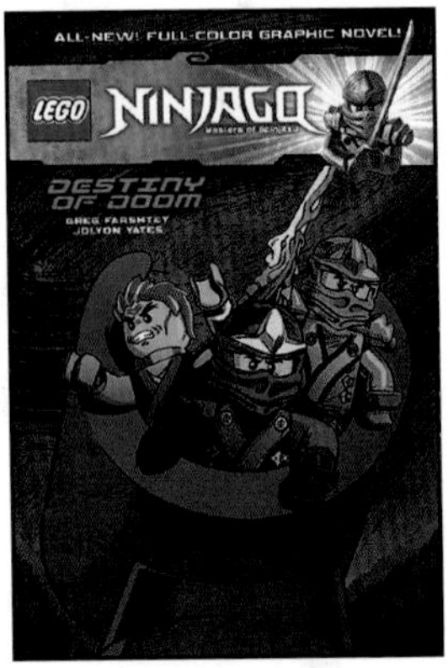
ALL-NEW! FULL-COLOR GRAPHIC NOVEL!
LEGO NINJAGO
DESTINY OF DOOM
GREG FARSHTEY JOLYON YATES
NINJAGO #8 (2 Jan 15)

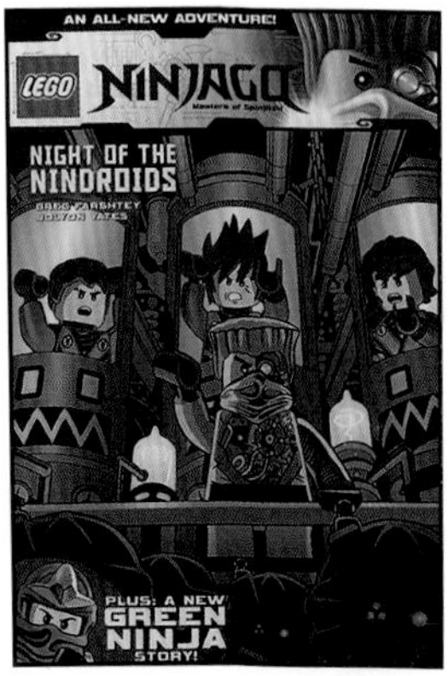
AN ALL-NEW ADVENTURE!
LEGO NINJAGO
NIGHT OF THE NINDROIDS
PLUS: A NEW GREEN NINJA STORY!
NINJAGO #9 (6 Feb 15)

TITAN COMICS

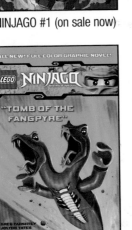

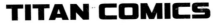

LEGO NINJAGO™
Masters of Spinjitzu

#3 RISE OF THE SERPENTINE

GREG FARSHTEY • Writer

PAUL LEE • Artist

LAURIE E. SMITH • Colourist

BRYAN SENKA • Letterer

TITAN
COMICS

LEGO® NINJAGO™ Masters of Spinjitzu
Volume Three: Rise of the Serpentine

Greg Farshtey – Writer
Paul Lee – Artist
Laurie E. Smith – Colourist
Bryan Senka – Letterer

Published by Titan Comics, a division of Titan Publishing Group Ltd., 144 Southwark St., London, SE1 0UP. LEGO NINJAGO: VOLUME #3: RISE OF THE SERPENTINE. LEGO, the LEGO logo and Ninjago are trademarks of the LEGO Group ©2014 The LEGO Group. All rights reserved. All characters, events and institutions depicted herein are fictional. Any similarity between any of the names, characters, persons, events and/or institutions in this publication to actual names, characters, and persons, whether living or dead and/or institutions are unintended and purely coincidental. License contact for Europe:Blue Ocean Entertainment AG, Germany.

A CIP catalogue record for this title is available from the British Library.

Printed in China.

First published in the USA and Canada in June 2013 by Papercutz.

10 9 8 7 6 5 4 3 2 1

ISBN: 9781782761945

www.titan-comics.com

www.LEGO.com

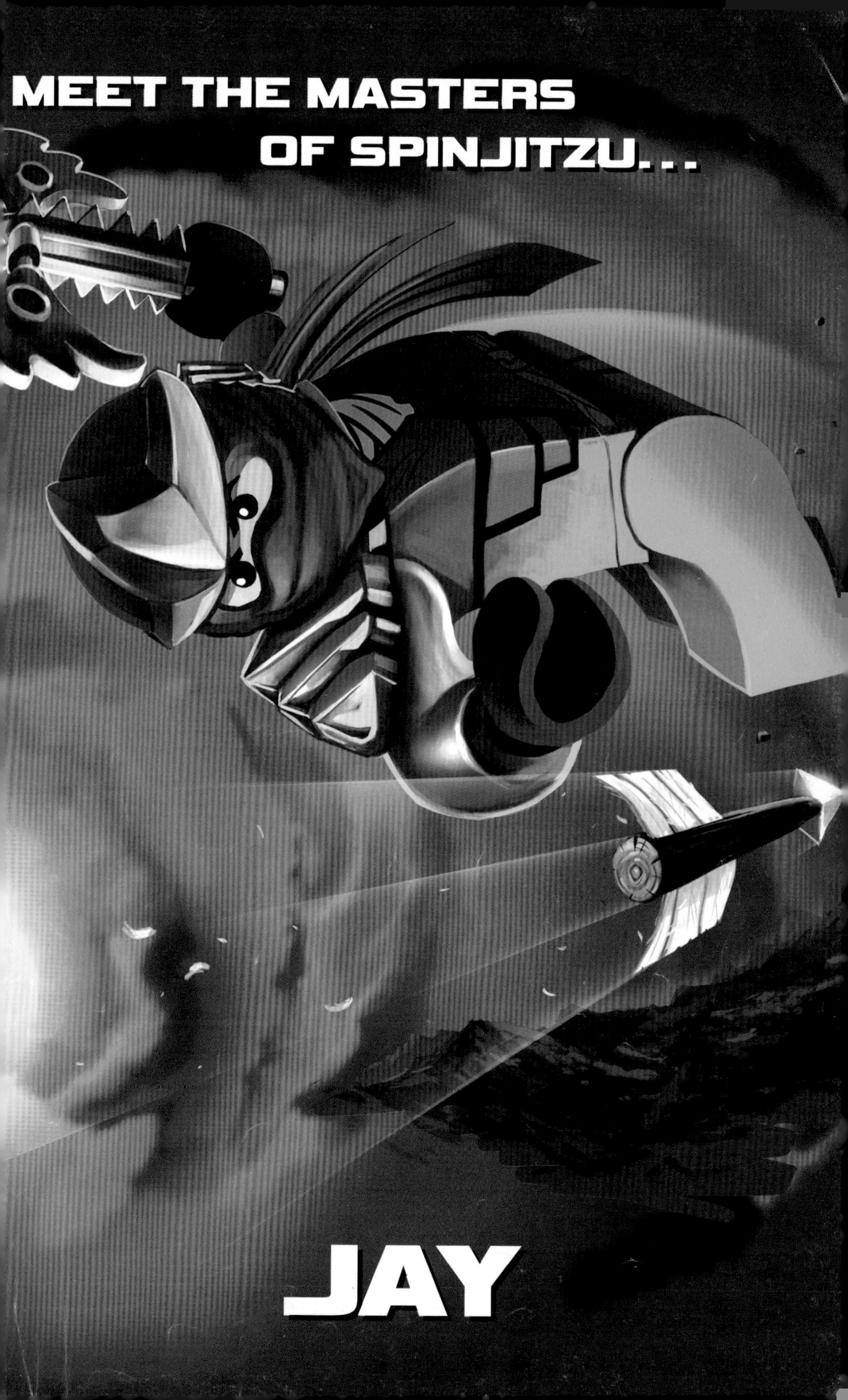
MEET THE MASTERS
OF SPINJITZU...
JAY

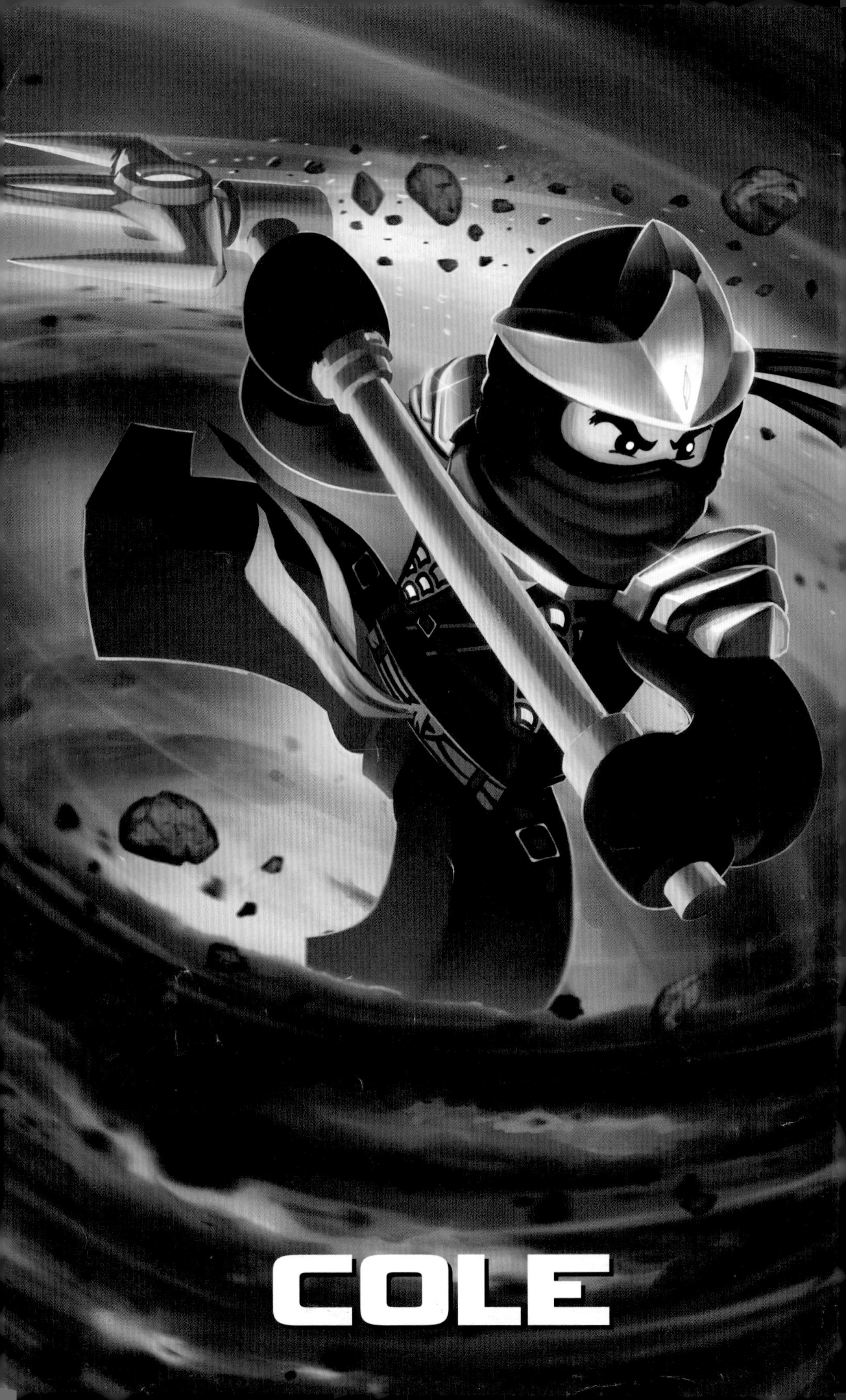
COLE

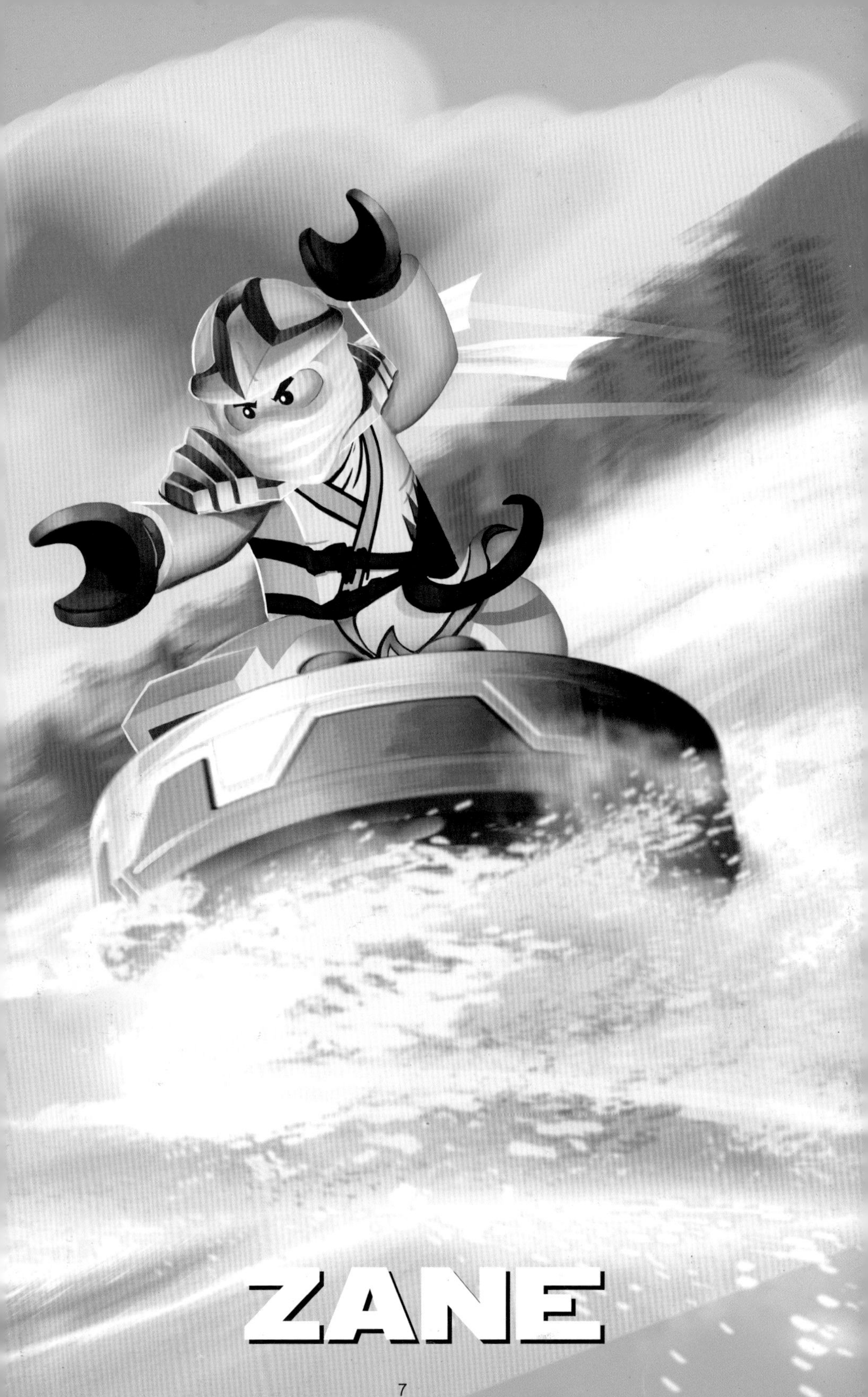

ZANE

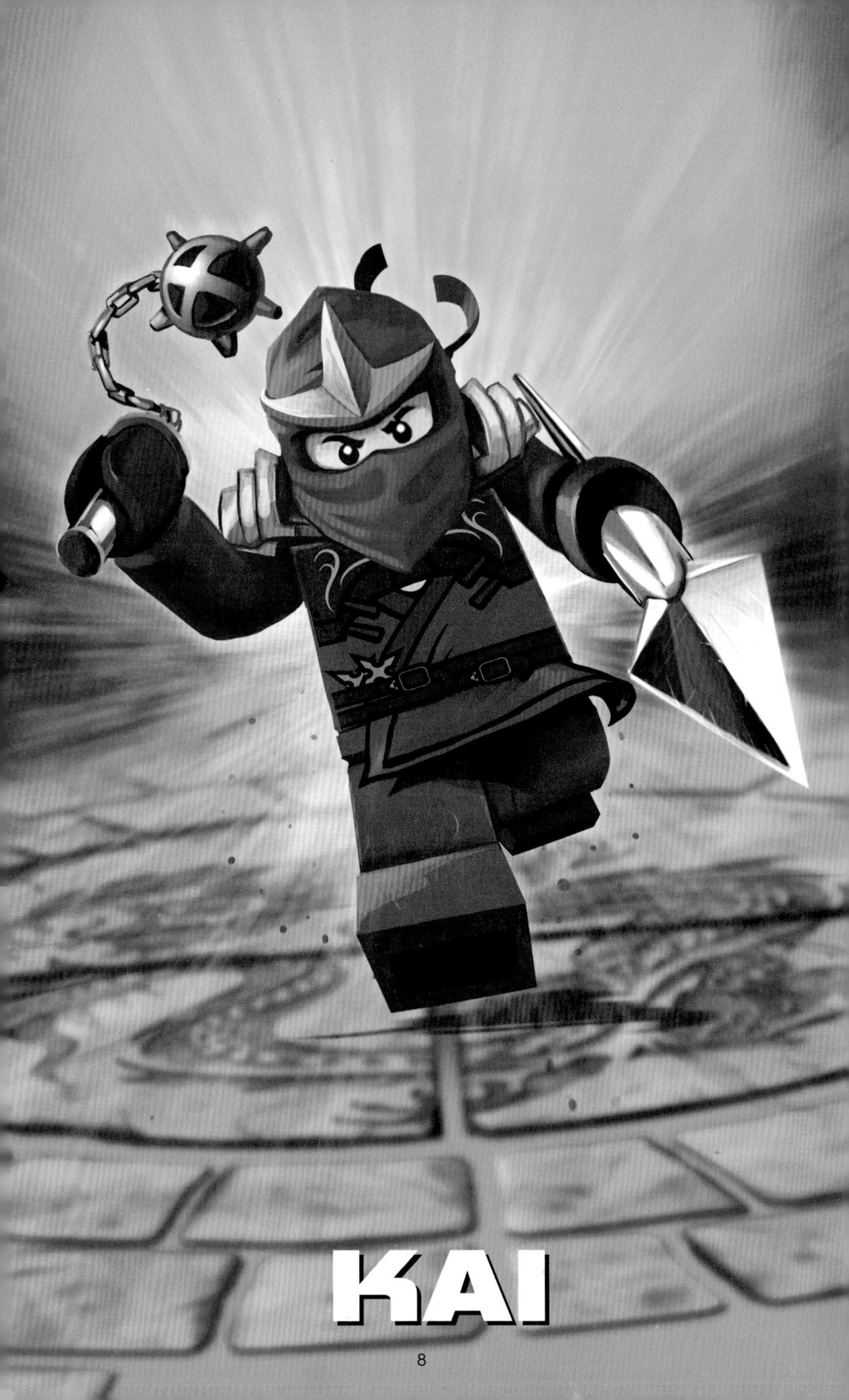

KAI

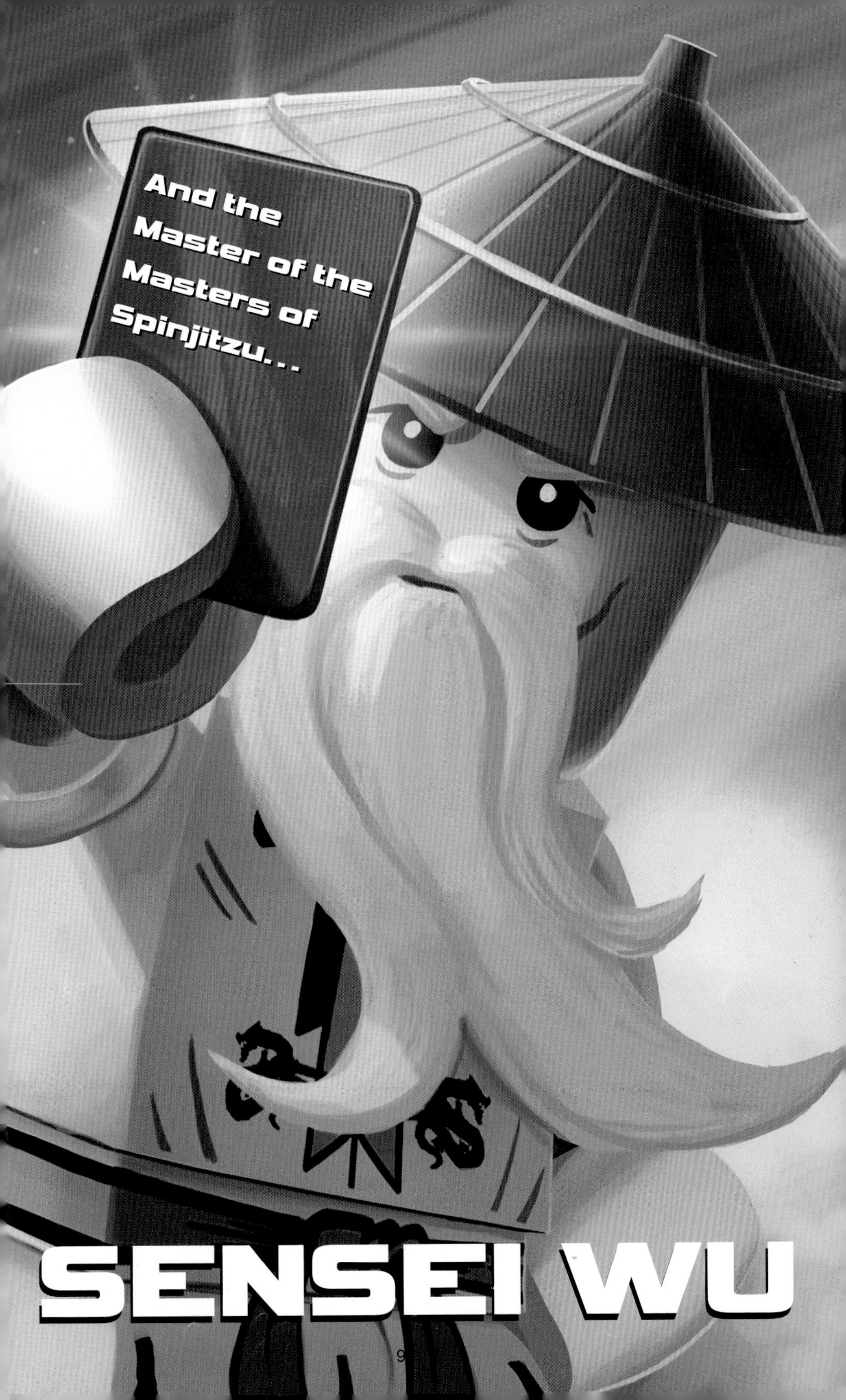

And the Master of the Masters of Spinjitzu...
SENSEI WU

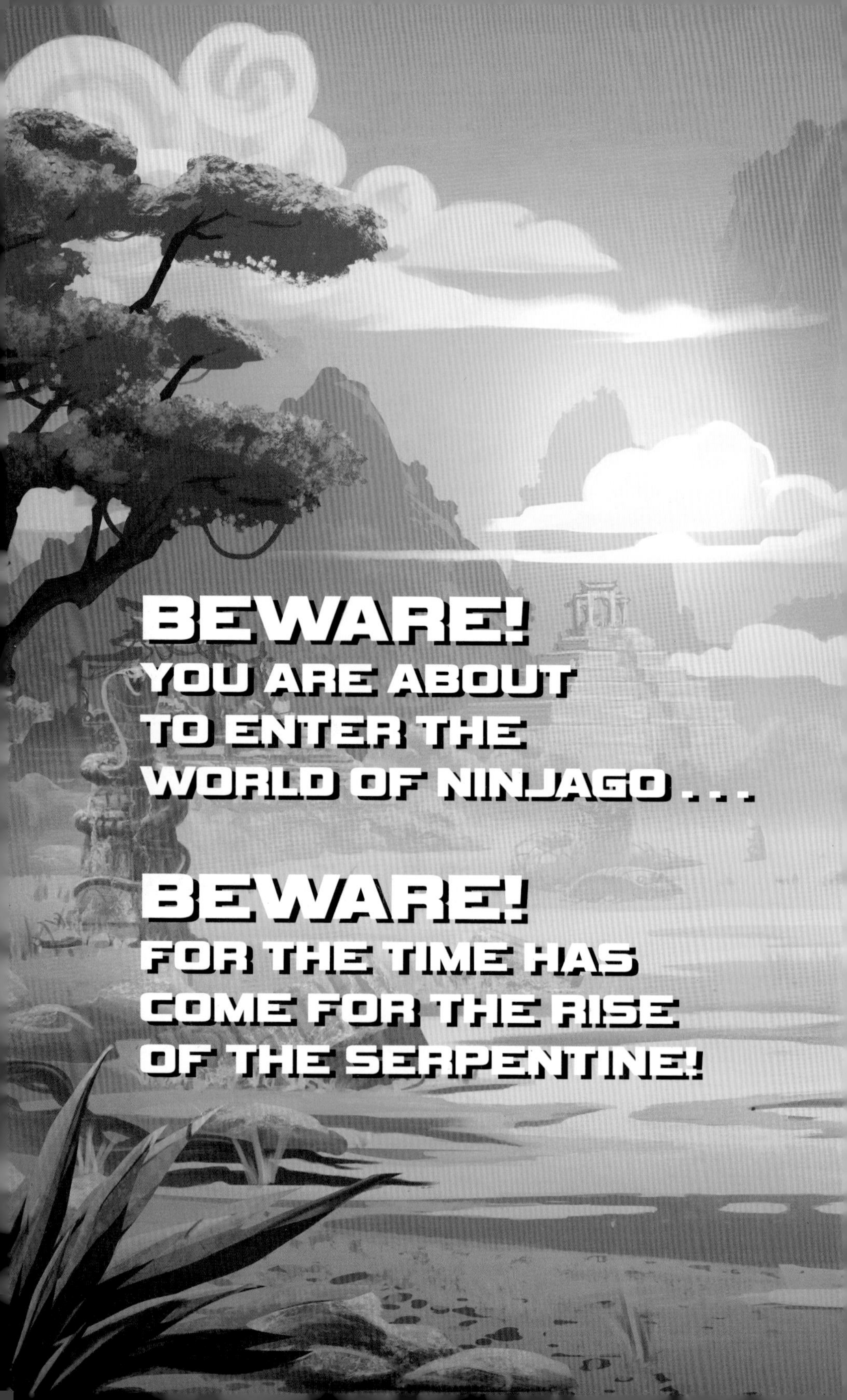
BEWARE!
YOU ARE ABOUT
TO ENTER THE
WORLD OF NINJAGO . . .
BEWARE!
FOR THE TIME HAS
COME FOR THE RISE
OF THE SERPENTINE!

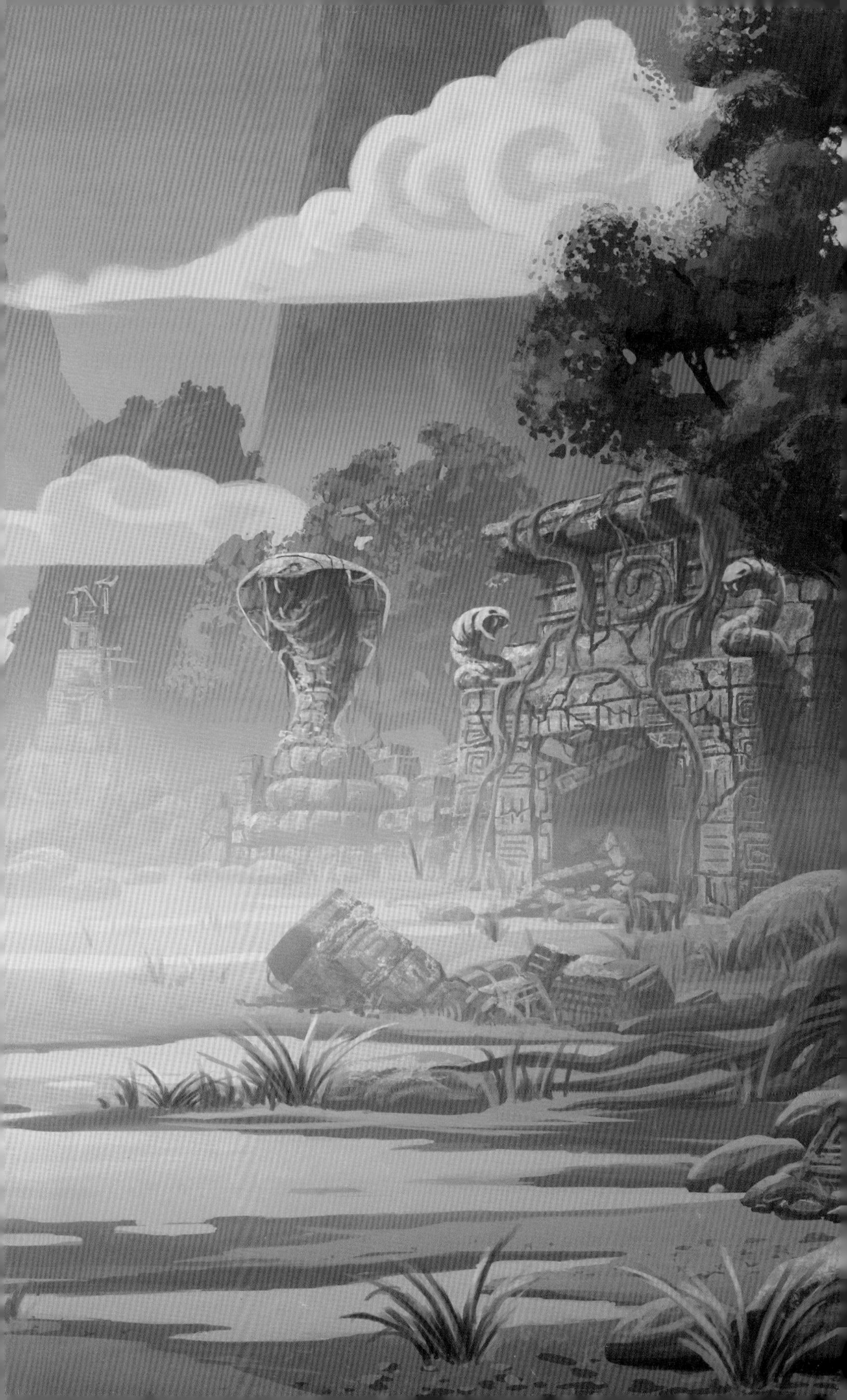

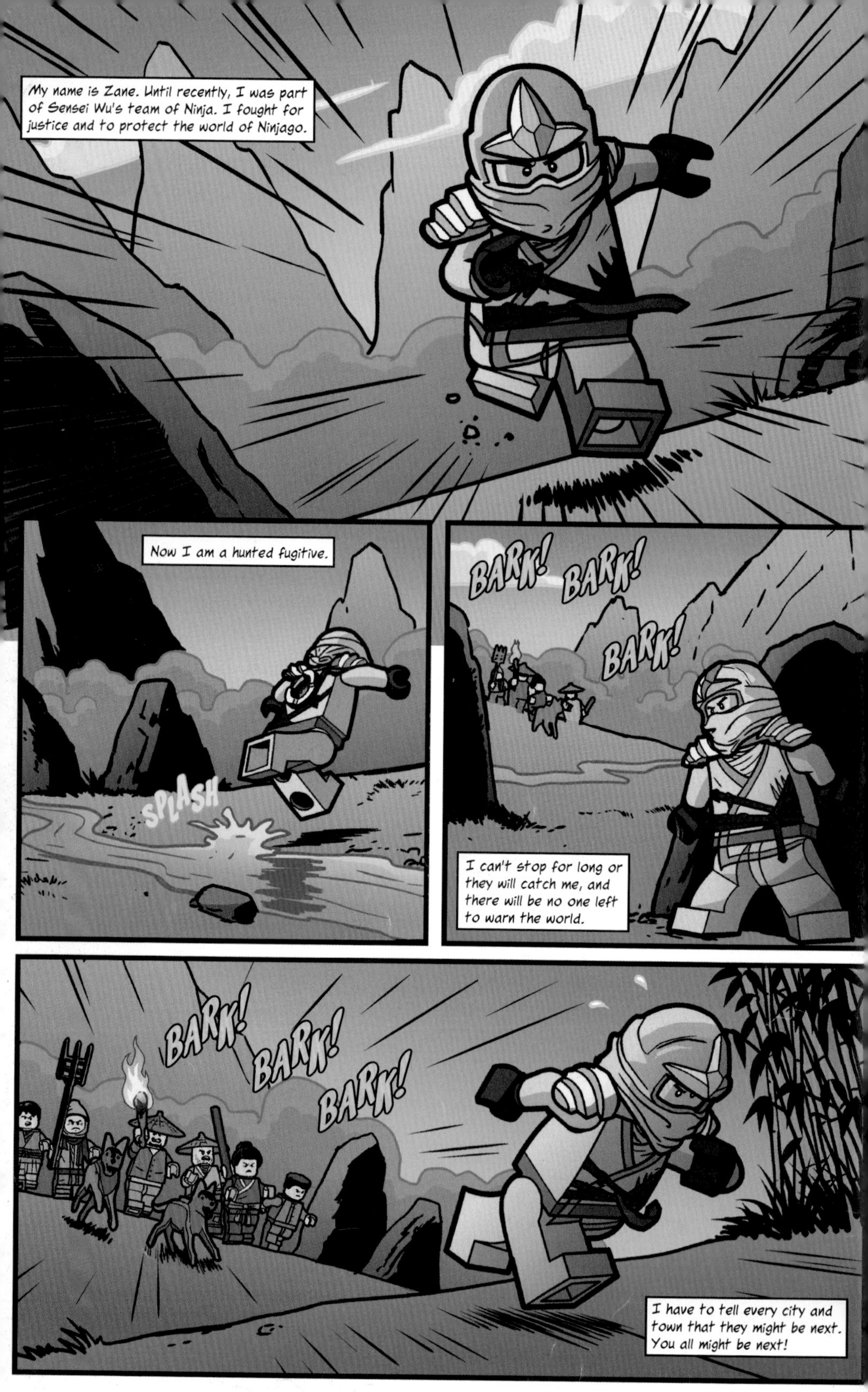
My name is Zane. Until recently, I was part of Sensei Wu's team of Ninja. I fought for justice and to protect the world of Ninjago.
Now I am a hunted fugitive.
SPLASH
BARK! BARK!
BARK!
I can't stop for long or they will catch me, and there will be no one left to warn the world.
BARK! BARK! BARK!
I have to tell every city and town that they might be next. You all might be next!

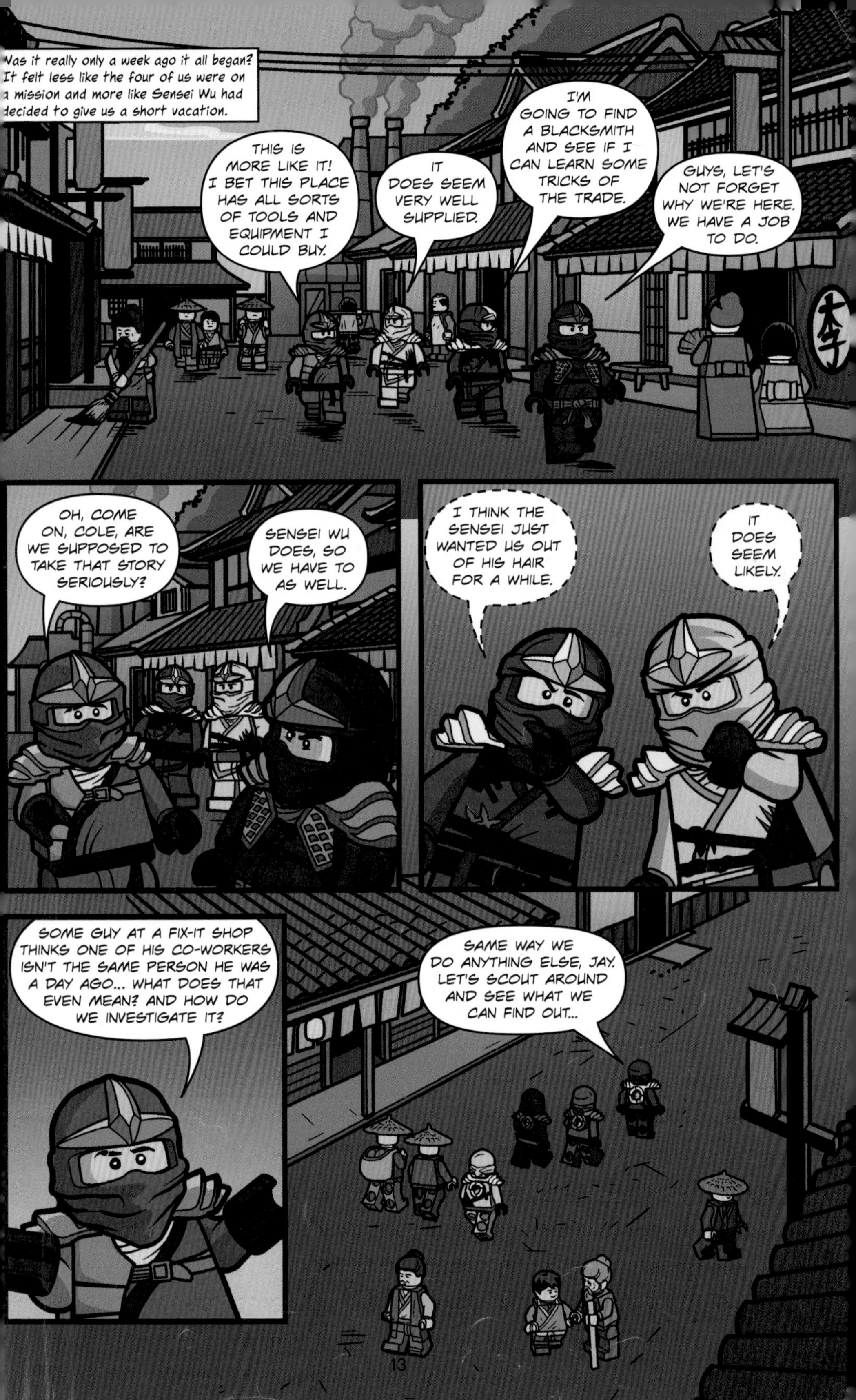
Was it really only a week ago it all began? It felt less like the four of us were on a mission and more like Sensei Wu had decided to give us a short vacation.
THIS IS MORE LIKE IT! I BET THIS PLACE HAS ALL SORTS OF TOOLS AND EQUIPMENT I COULD BUY.
IT DOES SEEM VERY WELL SUPPLIED.
I'M GOING TO FIND A BLACKSMITH AND SEE IF I CAN LEARN SOME TRICKS OF THE TRADE.
GUYS, LET'S NOT FORGET WHY WE'RE HERE. WE HAVE A JOB TO DO.
OH, COME ON, COLE, ARE WE SUPPOSED TO TAKE THAT STORY SERIOUSLY?
SENSEI WU DOES, SO WE HAVE TO AS WELL.
I THINK THE SENSEI JUST WANTED US OUT OF HIS HAIR FOR A WHILE.
IT DOES SEEM LIKELY.
SOME GUY AT A FIX-IT SHOP THINKS ONE OF HIS CO-WORKERS ISN'T THE SAME PERSON HE WAS A DAY AGO... WHAT DOES THAT EVEN MEAN? AND HOW DO WE INVESTIGATE IT?
SAME WAY WE DO ANYTHING ELSE, JAY. LET'S SCOUT AROUND AND SEE WHAT WE CAN FIND OUT...

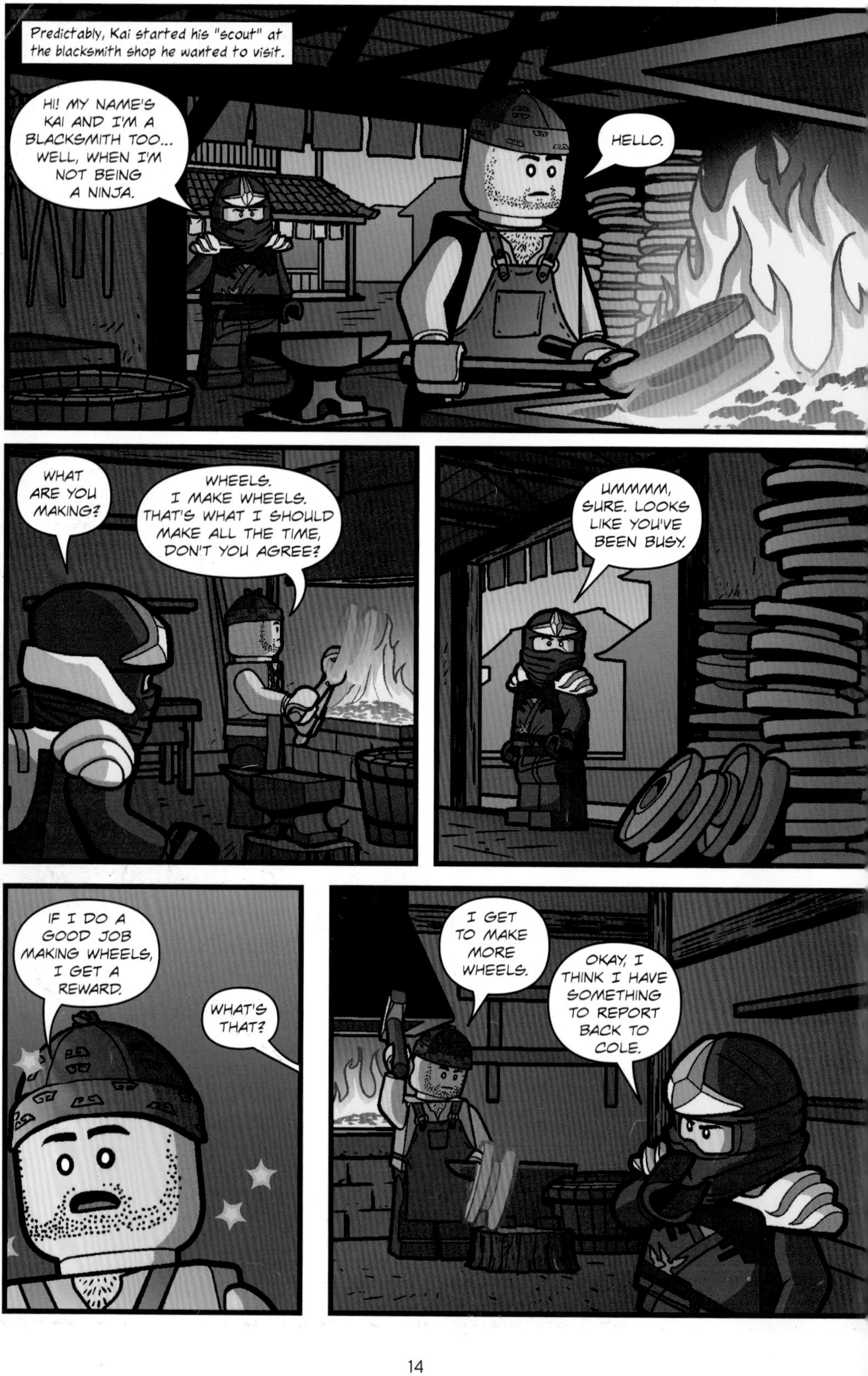
Predictably, Kai started his "scout" at the blacksmith shop he wanted to visit.
HI! MY NAME'S KAI AND I'M A BLACKSMITH TOO... WELL, WHEN I'M NOT BEING A NINJA.
HELLO.
WHAT ARE YOU MAKING?
WHEELS. I MAKE WHEELS. THAT'S WHAT I SHOULD MAKE ALL THE TIME, DON'T YOU AGREE?
UMMMM, SURE. LOOKS LIKE YOU'VE BEEN BUSY.
IF I DO A GOOD JOB MAKING WHEELS, I GET A REWARD.
WHAT'S THAT?
I GET TO MAKE MORE WHEELS.
OKAY, I THINK I HAVE SOMETHING TO REPORT BACK TO COLE.

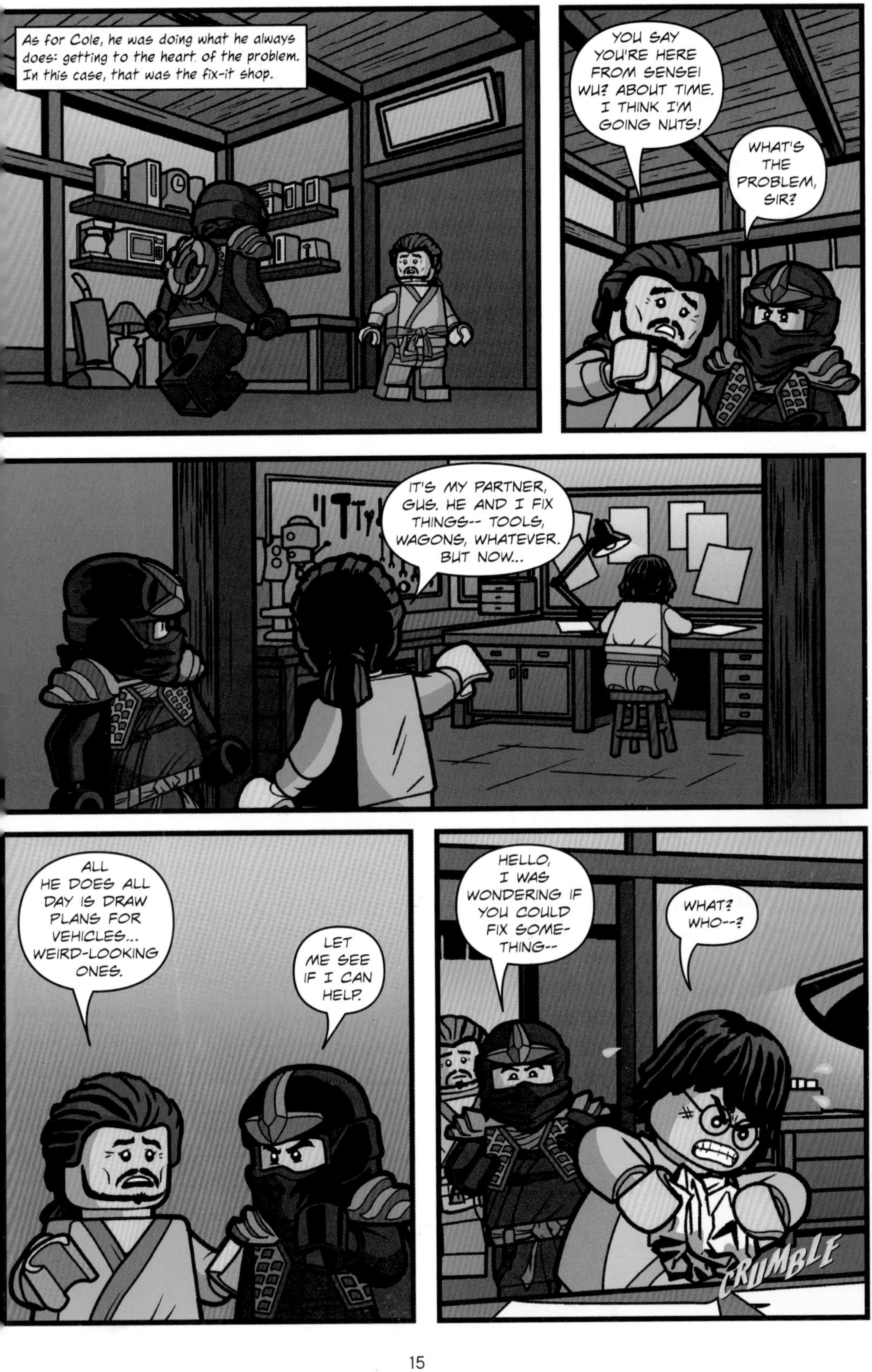
As for Cole, he was doing what he always does: getting to the heart of the problem. In this case, that was the fix-it shop.
YOU SAY YOU'RE HERE FROM SENSEI WU? ABOUT TIME. I THINK I'M GOING NUTS!
WHAT'S THE PROBLEM, SIR?
IT'S MY PARTNER, GUS. HE AND I FIX THINGS-- TOOLS, WAGONS, WHATEVER. BUT NOW...
ALL HE DOES ALL DAY IS DRAW PLANS FOR VEHICLES... WEIRD-LOOKING ONES.
LET ME SEE IF I CAN HELP.
HELLO, I WAS WONDERING IF YOU COULD FIX SOME-THING--
WHAT? WHO--?
CRUMBLE

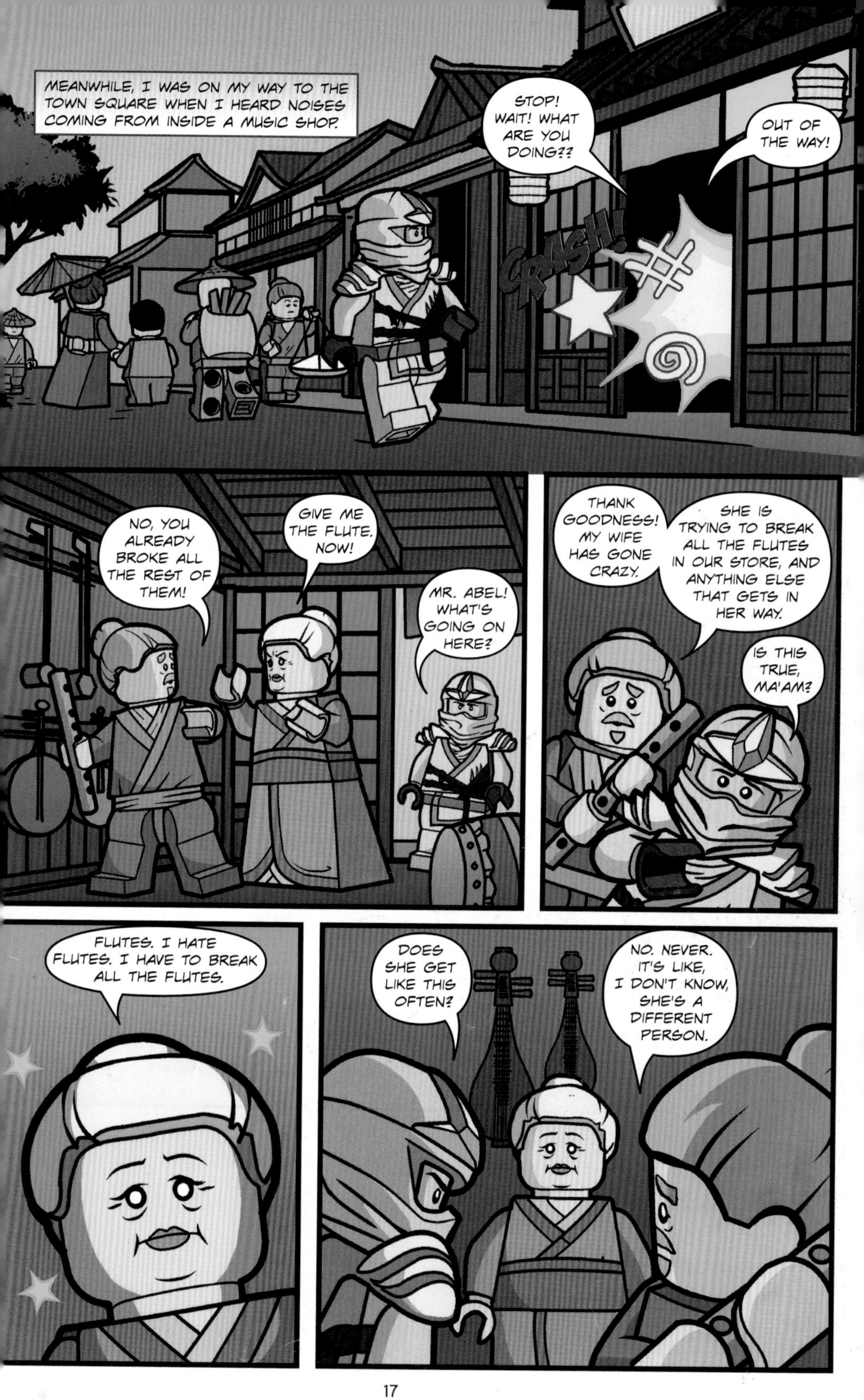
MEANWHILE, I WAS ON MY WAY TO THE TOWN SQUARE WHEN I HEARD NOISES COMING FROM INSIDE A MUSIC SHOP.
STOP! WAIT! WHAT ARE YOU DOING??
OUT OF THE WAY!
CRASH!
NO, YOU ALREADY BROKE ALL THE REST OF THEM!
GIVE ME THE FLUTE. NOW!
MR. ABEL! WHAT'S GOING ON HERE?
THANK GOODNESS! MY WIFE HAS GONE CRAZY.
SHE IS TRYING TO BREAK ALL THE FLUTES IN OUR STORE, AND ANYTHING ELSE THAT GETS IN HER WAY.
IS THIS TRUE, MA'AM?
FLUTES. I HATE FLUTES. I HAVE TO BREAK ALL THE FLUTES.
DOES SHE GET LIKE THIS OFTEN?
NO. NEVER. IT'S LIKE, I DON'T KNOW, SHE'S A DIFFERENT PERSON.

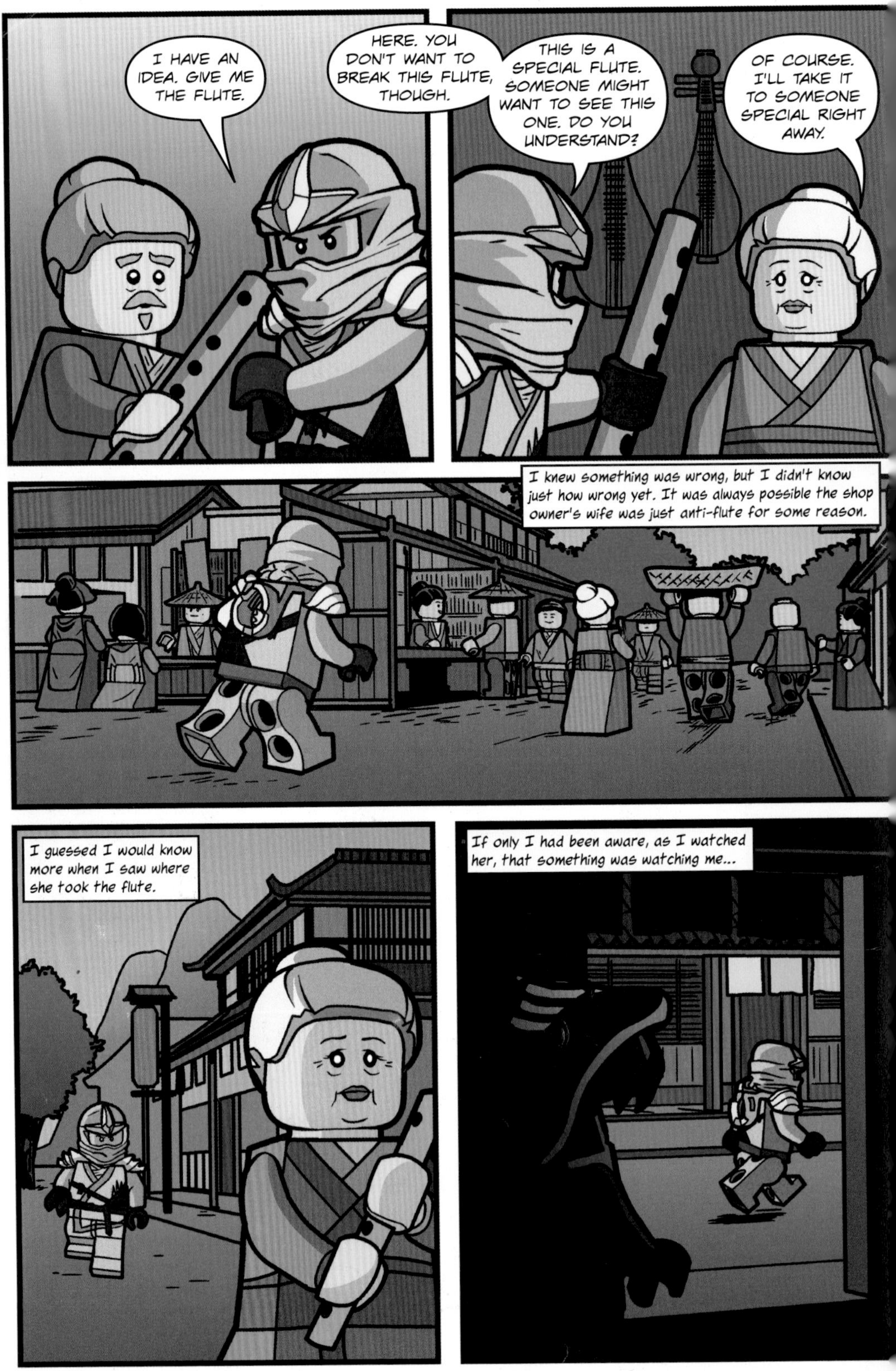
I HAVE AN IDEA. GIVE ME THE FLUTE.
HERE. YOU DON'T WANT TO BREAK THIS FLUTE, THOUGH.
THIS IS A SPECIAL FLUTE. SOMEONE MIGHT WANT TO SEE THIS ONE. DO YOU UNDERSTAND?
OF COURSE. I'LL TAKE IT TO SOMEONE SPECIAL RIGHT AWAY.
I knew something was wrong, but I didn't know just how wrong yet. It was always possible the shop owner's wife was just anti-flute for some reason.
I guessed I would know more when I saw where she took the flute.
If only I had been aware, as I watched her, that something was watching me...

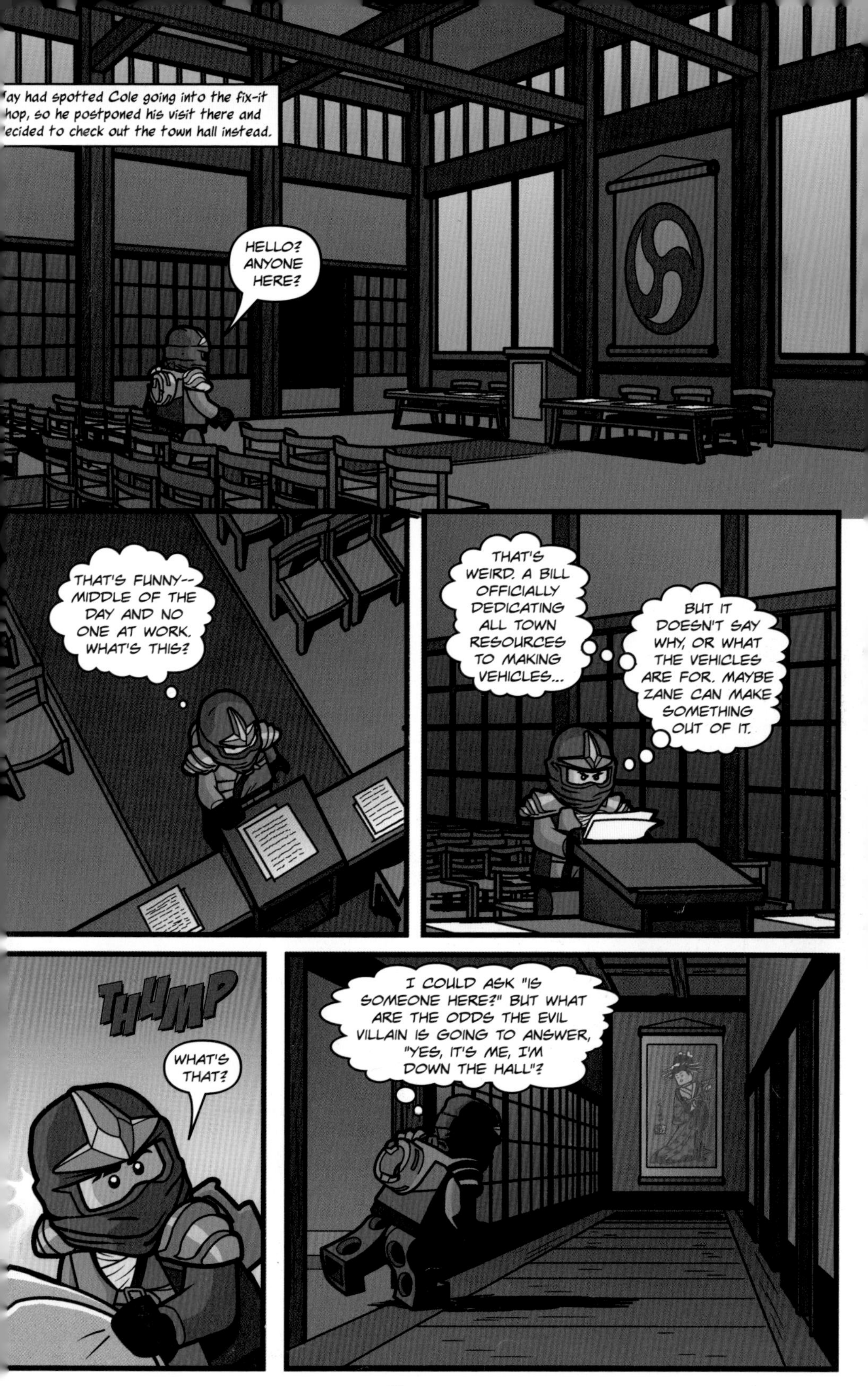
ay had spotted Cole going into the fix-it
hop, so he postponed his visit there and
ecided to check out the town hall instead.
HELLO? ANYONE HERE?
THAT'S FUNNY-- MIDDLE OF THE DAY AND NO ONE AT WORK. WHAT'S THIS?
THAT'S WEIRD. A BILL OFFICIALLY DEDICATING ALL TOWN RESOURCES TO MAKING VEHICLES...
BUT IT DOESN'T SAY WHY, OR WHAT THE VEHICLES ARE FOR. MAYBE ZANE CAN MAKE SOMETHING OUT OF IT.
THUMP
WHAT'S THAT?
I COULD ASK "IS SOMEONE HERE?" BUT WHAT ARE THE ODDS THE EVIL VILLAIN IS GOING TO ANSWER, "YES, IT'S ME, I'M DOWN THE HALL"?

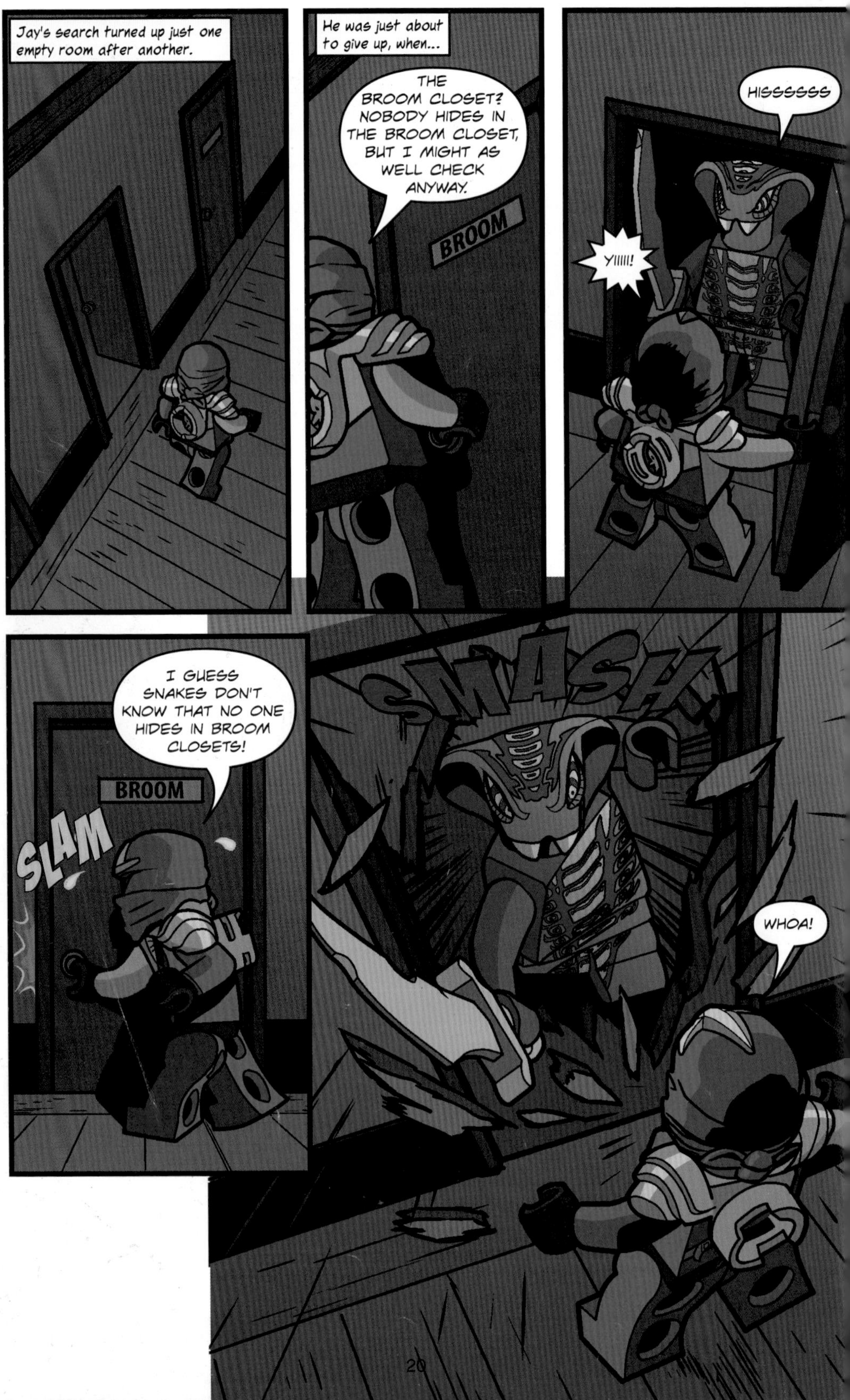
Jay's search turned up just one empty room after another.
He was just about to give up, when...
THE BROOM CLOSET? NOBODY HIDES IN THE BROOM CLOSET, BUT I MIGHT AS WELL CHECK ANYWAY.
BROOM
HISSSSSS
YIIIII!
I GUESS SNAKES DON'T KNOW THAT NO ONE HIDES IN BROOM CLOSETS!
BROOM
SLAM
SMASH
WHOA!

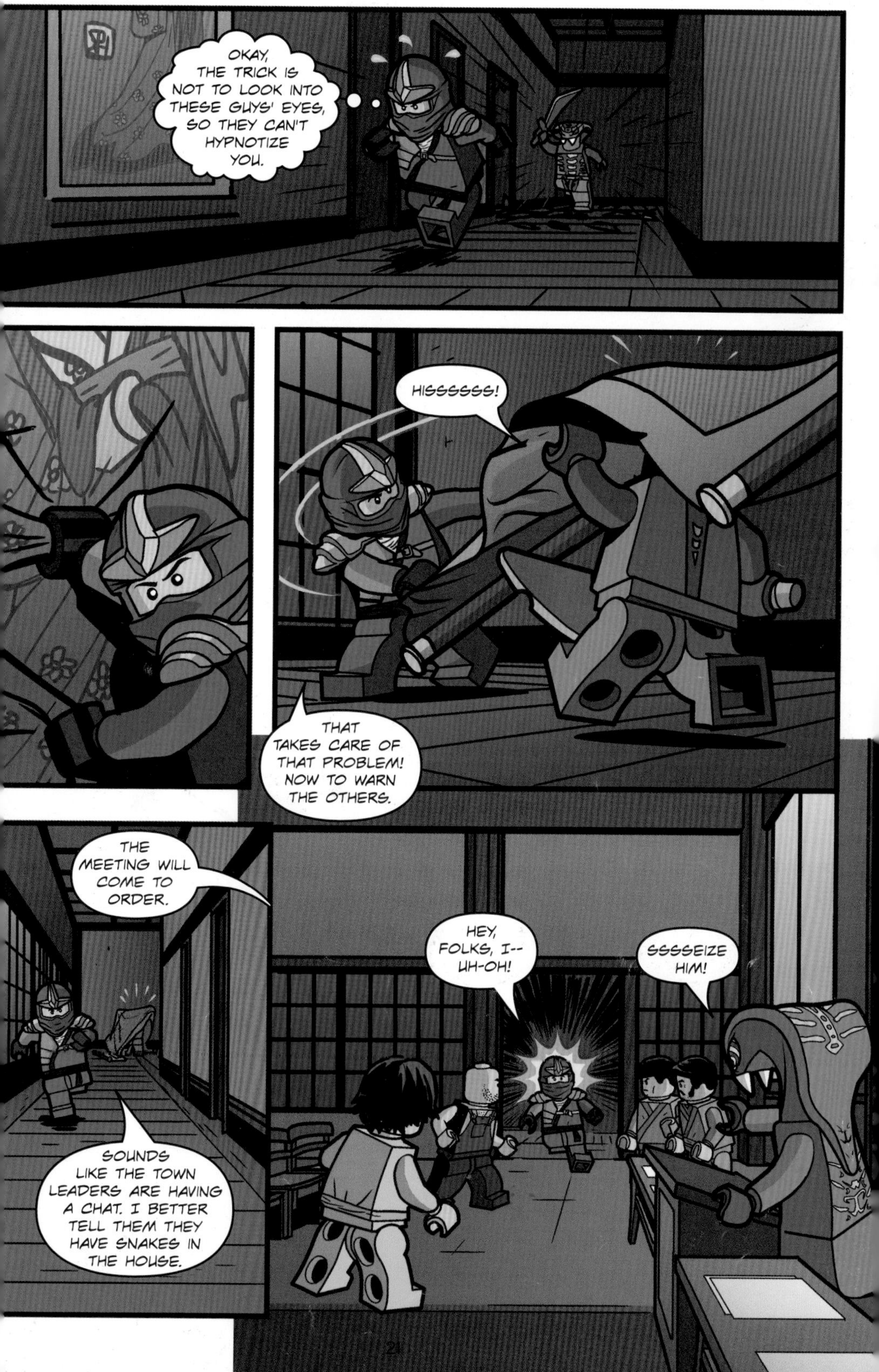
OKAY, THE TRICK IS NOT TO LOOK INTO THESE GUYS' EYES, SO THEY CAN'T HYPNOTIZE YOU.
HISSSSSS!
THAT TAKES CARE OF THAT PROBLEM! NOW TO WARN THE OTHERS.
THE MEETING WILL COME TO ORDER.
SOUNDS LIKE THE TOWN LEADERS ARE HAVING A CHAT. I BETTER TELL THEM THEY HAVE SNAKES IN THE HOUSE.
HEY, FOLKS, I-- UH-OH!
SSSSEIZE HIM!

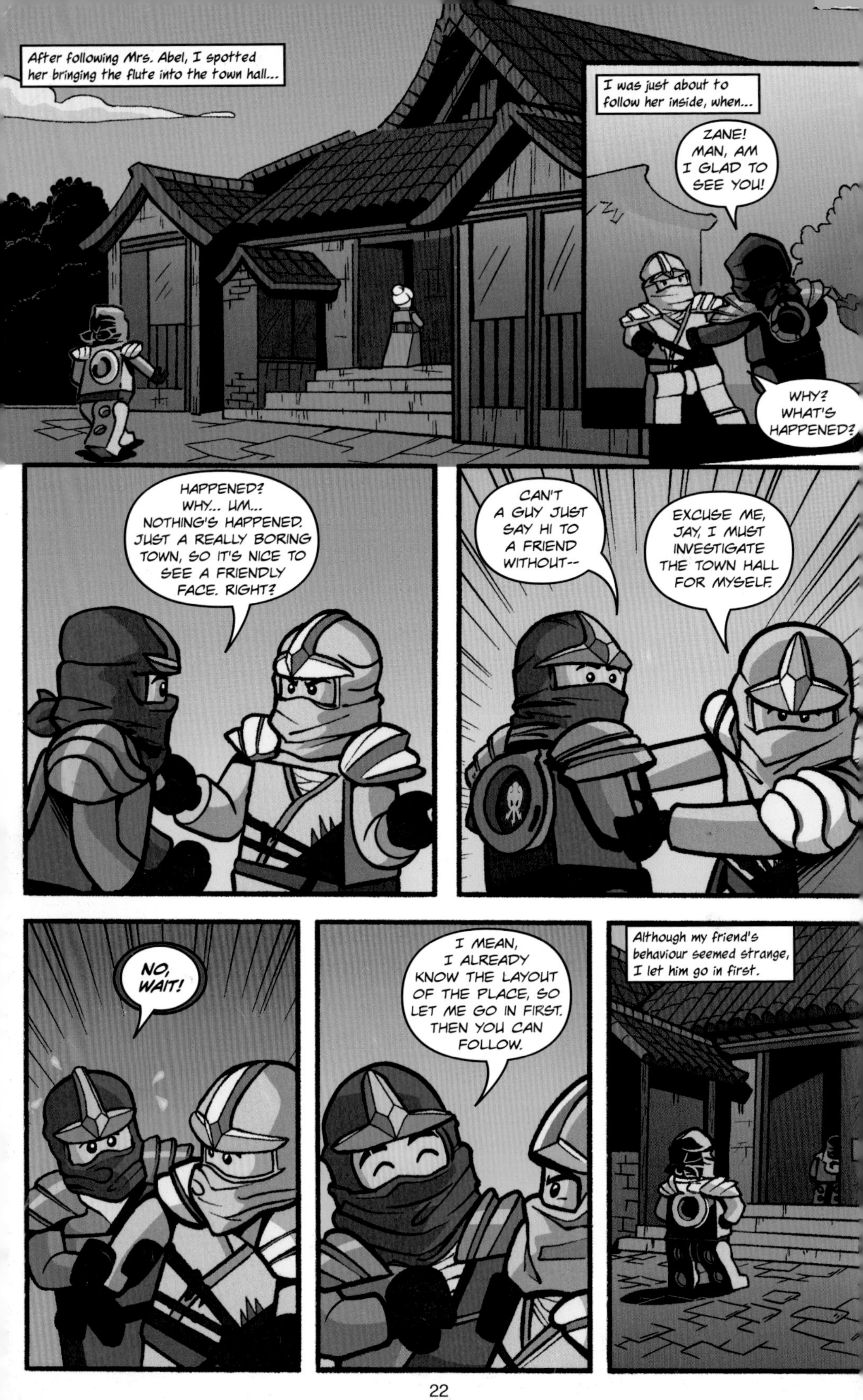
After following Mrs. Abel, I spotted her bringing the flute into the town hall...
I was just about to follow her inside, when...
ZANE! MAN, AM I GLAD TO SEE YOU!
WHY? WHAT'S HAPPENED?
HAPPENED? WHY... UM... NOTHING'S HAPPENED. JUST A REALLY BORING TOWN, SO IT'S NICE TO SEE A FRIENDLY FACE. RIGHT?
CAN'T A GUY JUST SAY HI TO A FRIEND WITHOUT--
EXCUSE ME, JAY, I MUST INVESTIGATE THE TOWN HALL FOR MYSELF.
NO, WAIT!
I MEAN, I ALREADY KNOW THE LAYOUT OF THE PLACE, SO LET ME GO IN FIRST. THEN YOU CAN FOLLOW.
Although my friend's behaviour seemed strange, I let him go in first.

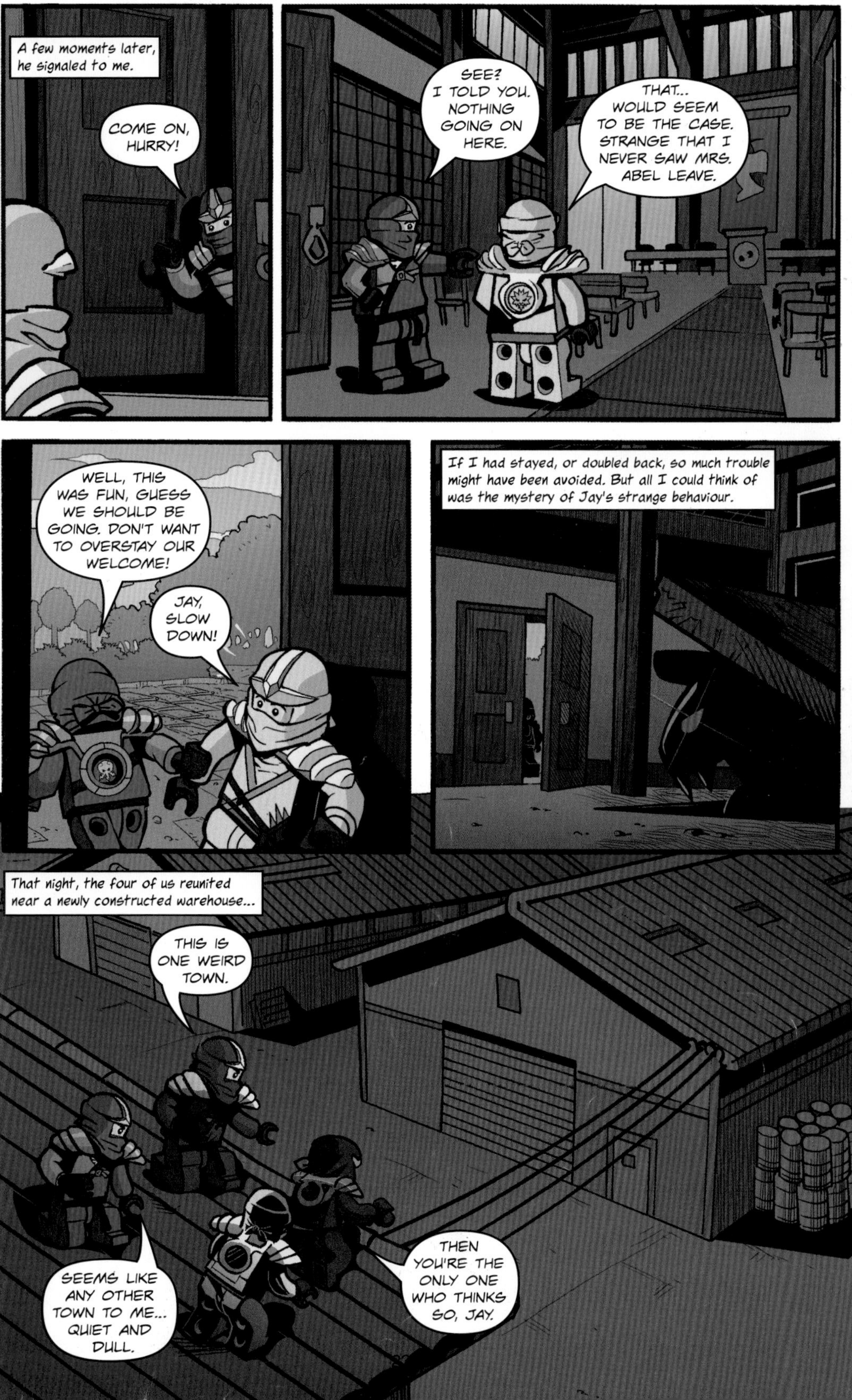
A few moments later, he signaled to me.
COME ON, HURRY!
SEE? I TOLD YOU. NOTHING GOING ON HERE.
THAT... WOULD SEEM TO BE THE CASE. STRANGE THAT I NEVER SAW MRS. ABEL LEAVE.
WELL, THIS WAS FUN, GUESS WE SHOULD BE GOING. DON'T WANT TO OVERSTAY OUR WELCOME!
JAY, SLOW DOWN!
If I had stayed, or doubled back, so much trouble might have been avoided. But all I could think of was the mystery of Jay's strange behaviour.
That night, the four of us reunited near a newly constructed warehouse...
THIS IS ONE WEIRD TOWN.
SEEMS LIKE ANY OTHER TOWN TO ME... QUIET AND DULL.
THEN YOU'RE THE ONLY ONE WHO THINKS SO, JAY.

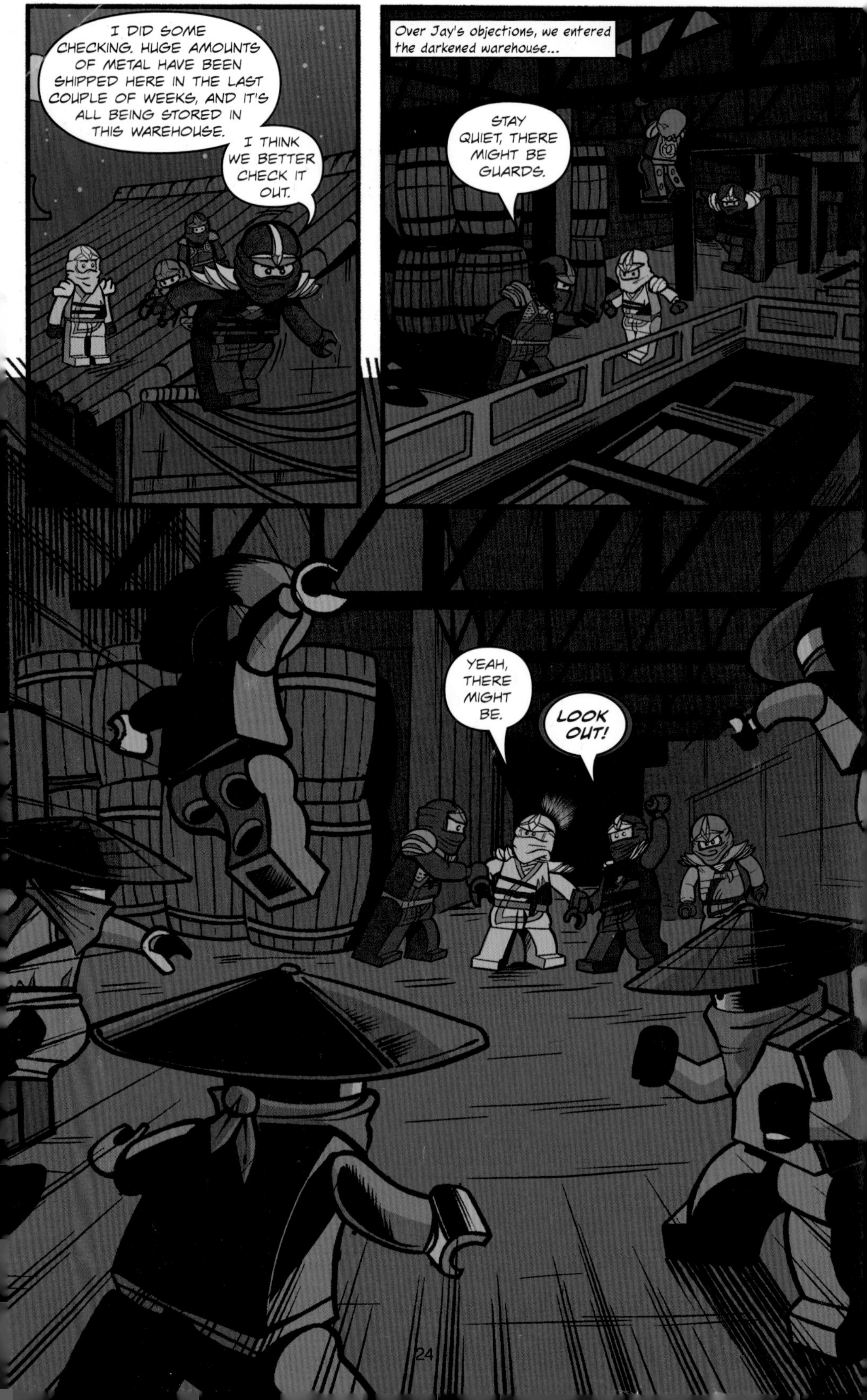
I DID SOME CHECKING. HUGE AMOUNTS OF METAL HAVE BEEN SHIPPED HERE IN THE LAST COUPLE OF WEEKS, AND IT'S ALL BEING STORED IN THIS WAREHOUSE.
I THINK WE BETTER CHECK IT OUT.
Over Jay's objections, we entered the darkened warehouse...
STAY QUIET, THERE MIGHT BE GUARDS.
YEAH, THERE MIGHT BE.
LOOK OUT!

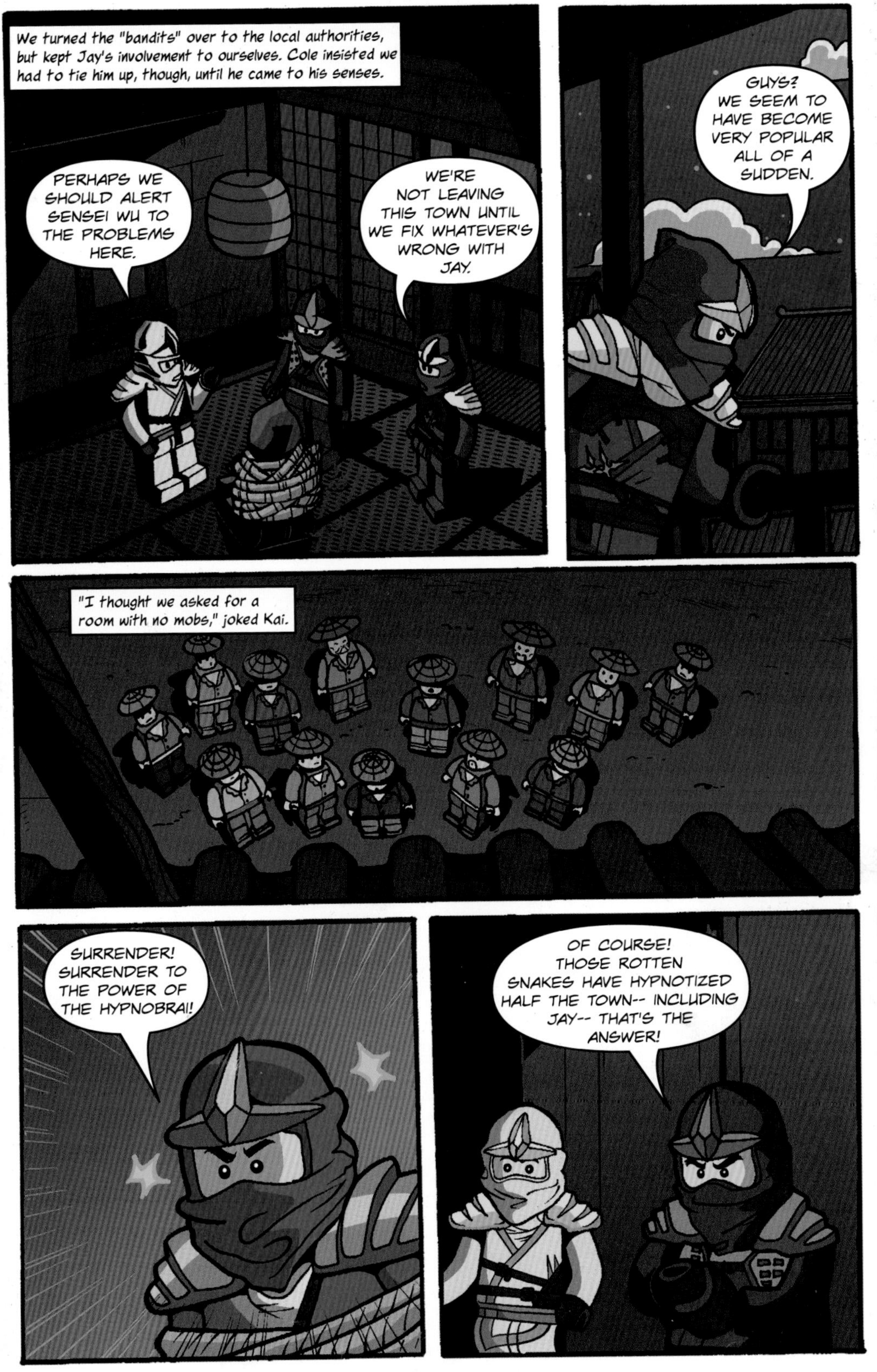

We turned the "bandits" over to the local authorities, but kept Jay's involvement to ourselves. Cole insisted we had to tie him up, though, until he came to his senses.
PERHAPS WE SHOULD ALERT SENSEI WU TO THE PROBLEMS HERE.
WE'RE NOT LEAVING THIS TOWN UNTIL WE FIX WHATEVER'S WRONG WITH JAY.
GUYS? WE SEEM TO HAVE BECOME VERY POPULAR ALL OF A SUDDEN.
"I thought we asked for a room with no mobs," joked Kai.
SURRENDER! SURRENDER TO THE POWER OF THE HYPNOBRAI!
OF COURSE! THOSE ROTTEN SNAKES HAVE HYPNOTIZED HALF THE TOWN-- INCLUDING JAY-- THAT'S THE ANSWER!

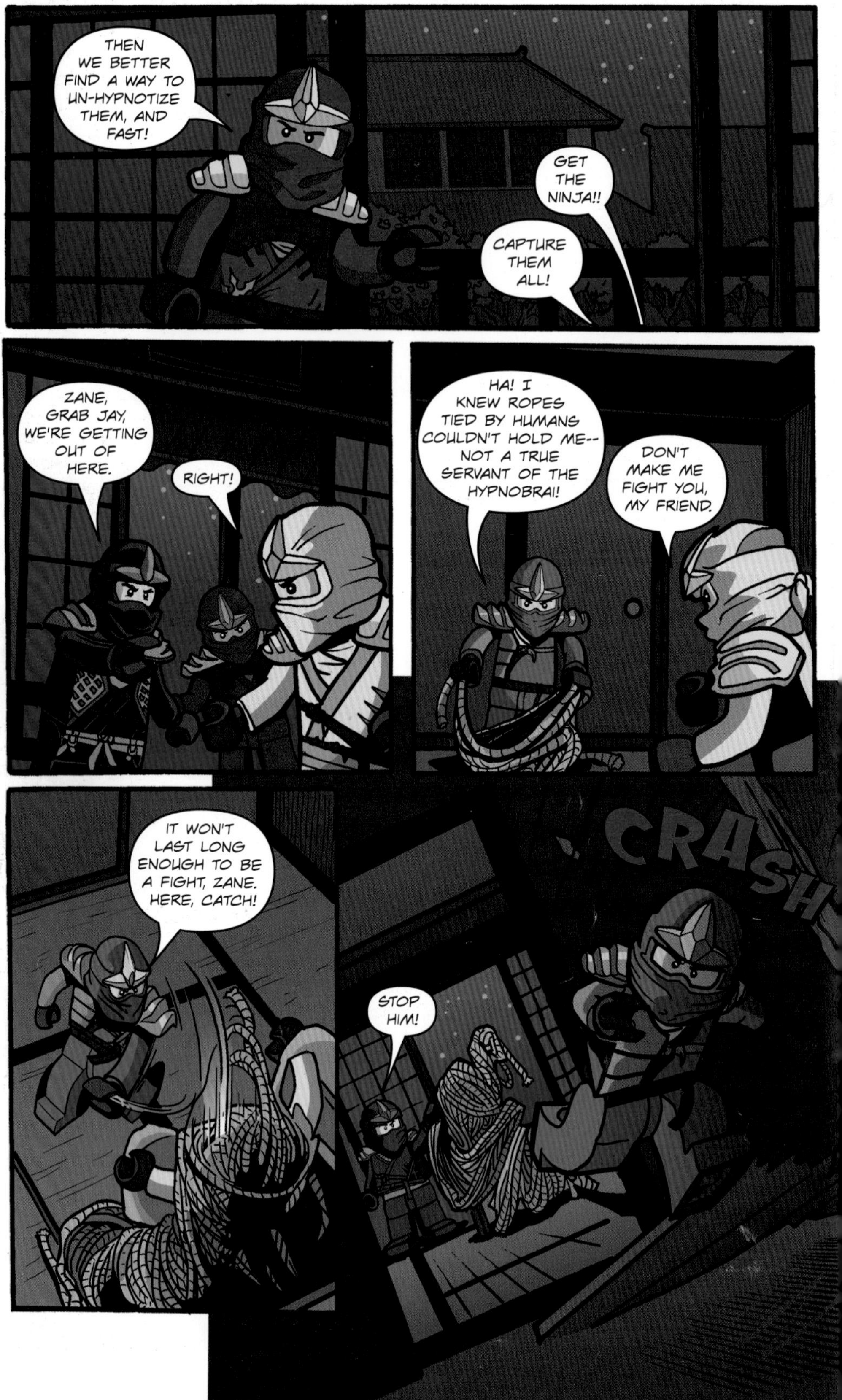
THEN WE BETTER FIND A WAY TO UN-HYPNOTIZE THEM, AND FAST!
GET THE NINJA!!
CAPTURE THEM ALL!
ZANE, GRAB JAY, WE'RE GETTING OUT OF HERE.
RIGHT!
HA! I KNEW ROPES TIED BY HUMANS COULDN'T HOLD ME-- NOT A TRUE SERVANT OF THE HYPNOBRAI!
DON'T MAKE ME FIGHT YOU, MY FRIEND.
IT WON'T LAST LONG ENOUGH TO BE A FIGHT, ZANE. HERE, CATCH!
CRASH
STOP HIM!

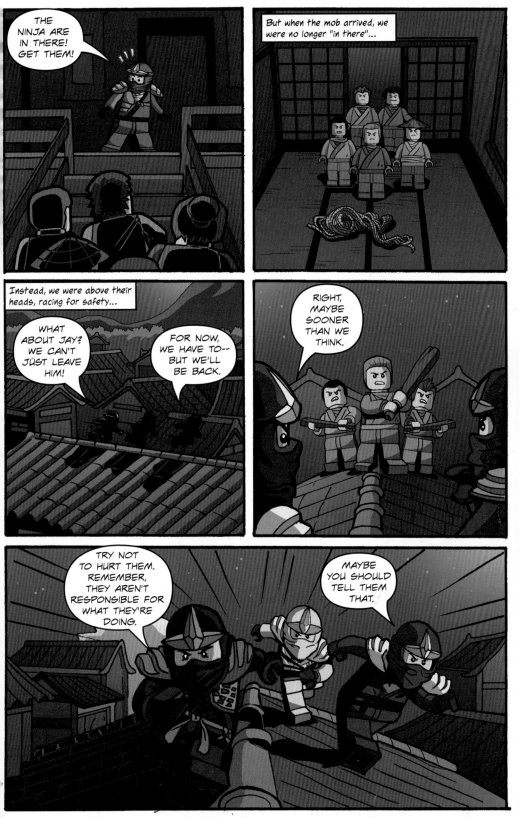

THE NINJA ARE IN THERE! GET THEM!

But when the mob arrived, we were no longer "in there"...

Instead, we were above their heads, racing for safety...

WHAT ABOUT JAY? WE CAN'T JUST LEAVE HIM!

FOR NOW, WE HAVE TO-- BUT WE'LL BE BACK.

RIGHT, MAYBE SOONER THAN WE THINK.

TRY NOT TO HURT THEM. REMEMBER, THEY AREN'T RESPONSIBLE FOR WHAT THEY'RE DOING.

MAYBE YOU SHOULD TELL THEM THAT.

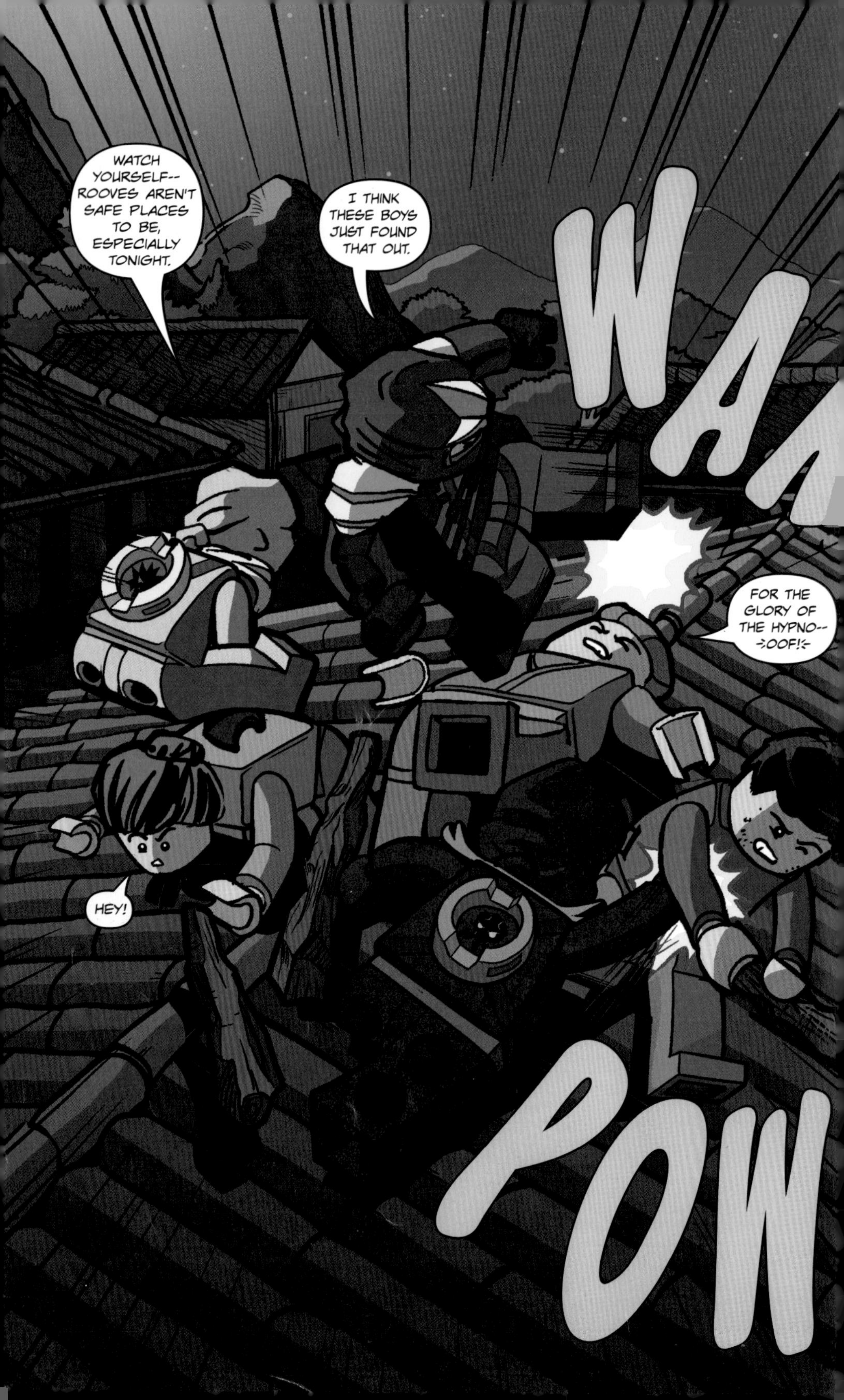
WATCH YOURSELF-- ROOVES AREN'T SAFE PLACES TO BE, ESPECIALLY TONIGHT.
I THINK THESE BOYS JUST FOUND THAT OUT.
WAM
FOR THE GLORY OF THE HYPNO-- -OOF!-
HEY!
POW

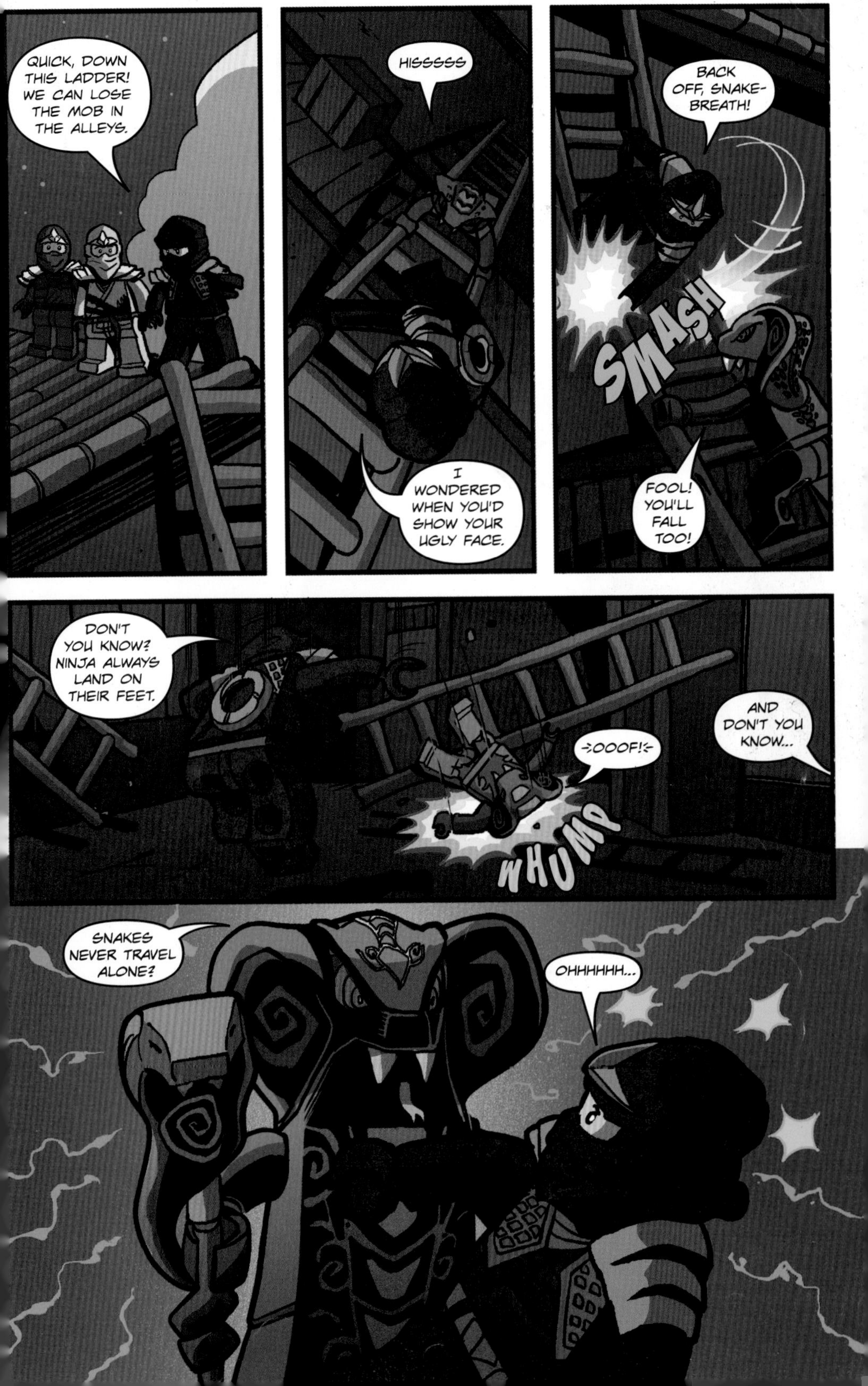
QUICK, DOWN THIS LADDER! WE CAN LOSE THE MOB IN THE ALLEYS.
HISSSSS
I WONDERED WHEN YOU'D SHOW YOUR UGLY FACE.
BACK OFF, SNAKE-BREATH!
SMASH
FOOL! YOU'LL FALL TOO!
DON'T YOU KNOW? NINJA ALWAYS LAND ON THEIR FEET.
OOOF!
AND DON'T YOU KNOW...
WHUMP
SNAKES NEVER TRAVEL ALONE?
OHHHHHH...

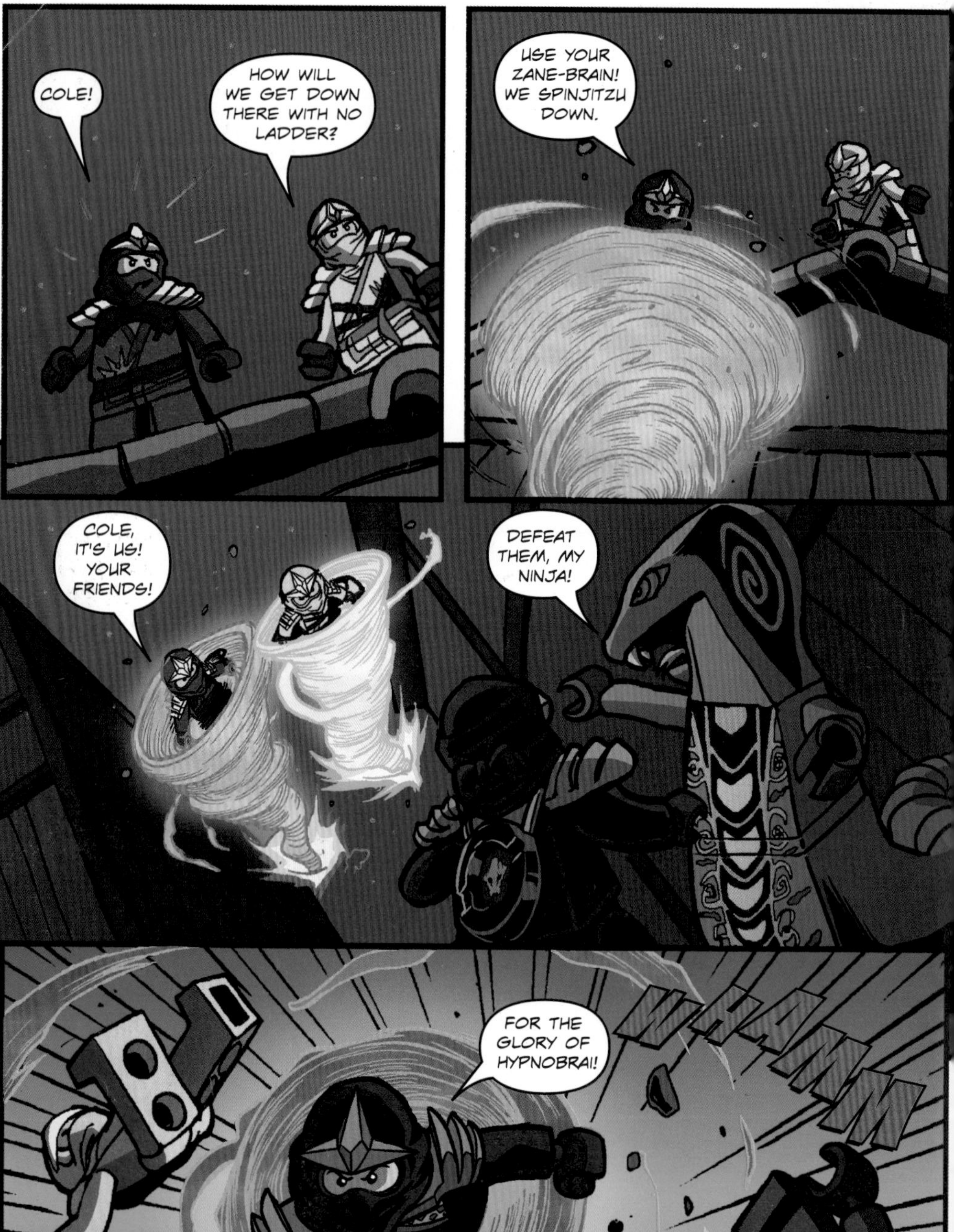
COLE!
HOW WILL WE GET DOWN THERE WITH NO LADDER?
USE YOUR ZANE-BRAIN! WE SPINJITZU DOWN.
COLE, IT'S US! YOUR FRIENDS!
DEFEAT THEM, MY NINJA!
FOR THE GLORY OF HYPNOBRAI!
WHAMM

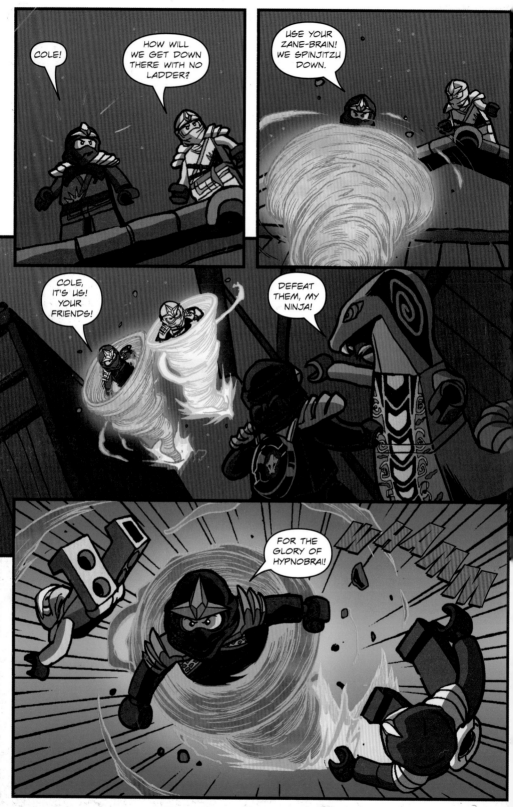

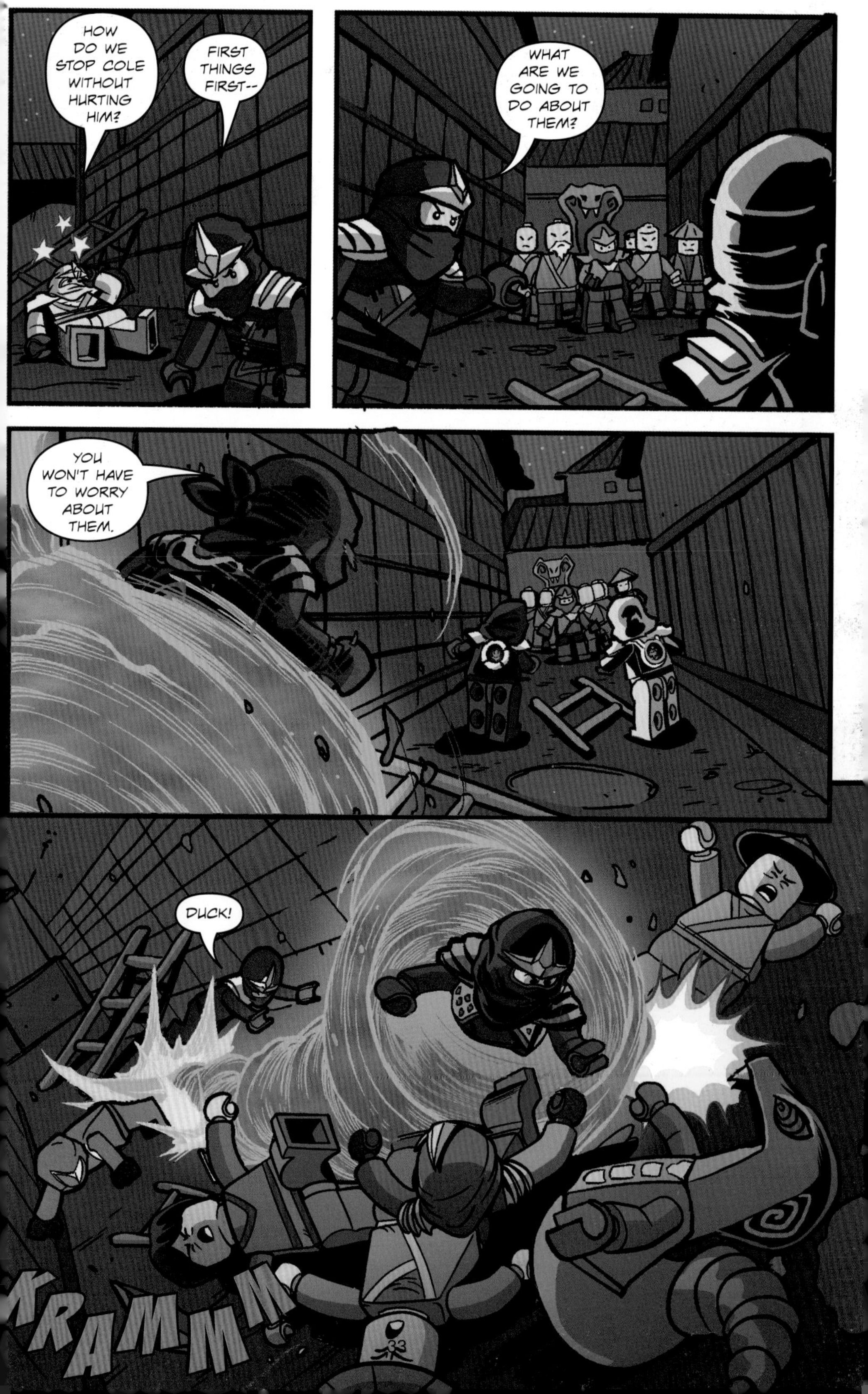
HOW DO WE STOP COLE WITHOUT HURTING HIM?
FIRST THINGS FIRST--
WHAT ARE WE GOING TO DO ABOUT THEM?
YOU WON'T HAVE TO WORRY ABOUT THEM.
DUCK!
KRAMMM

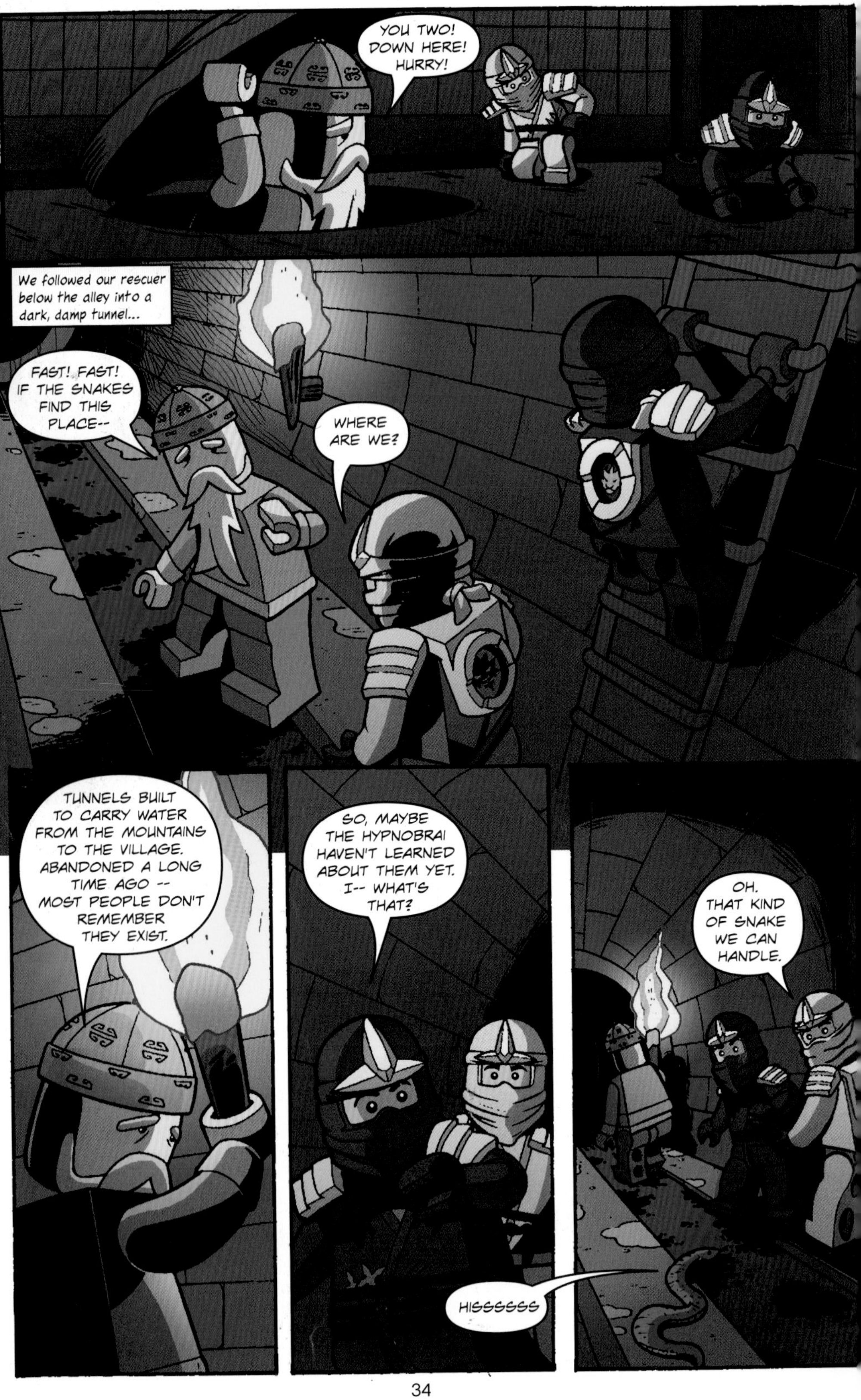
YOU TWO! DOWN HERE! HURRY!
We followed our rescuer below the alley into a dark, damp tunnel...
FAST! FAST! IF THE SNAKES FIND THIS PLACE--
WHERE ARE WE?
TUNNELS BUILT TO CARRY WATER FROM THE MOUNTAINS TO THE VILLAGE. ABANDONED A LONG TIME AGO -- MOST PEOPLE DON'T REMEMBER THEY EXIST.
SO, MAYBE THE HYPNOBRAI HAVEN'T LEARNED ABOUT THEM YET. I-- WHAT'S THAT?
HISSSSSS
OH. THAT KIND OF SNAKE WE CAN HANDLE.

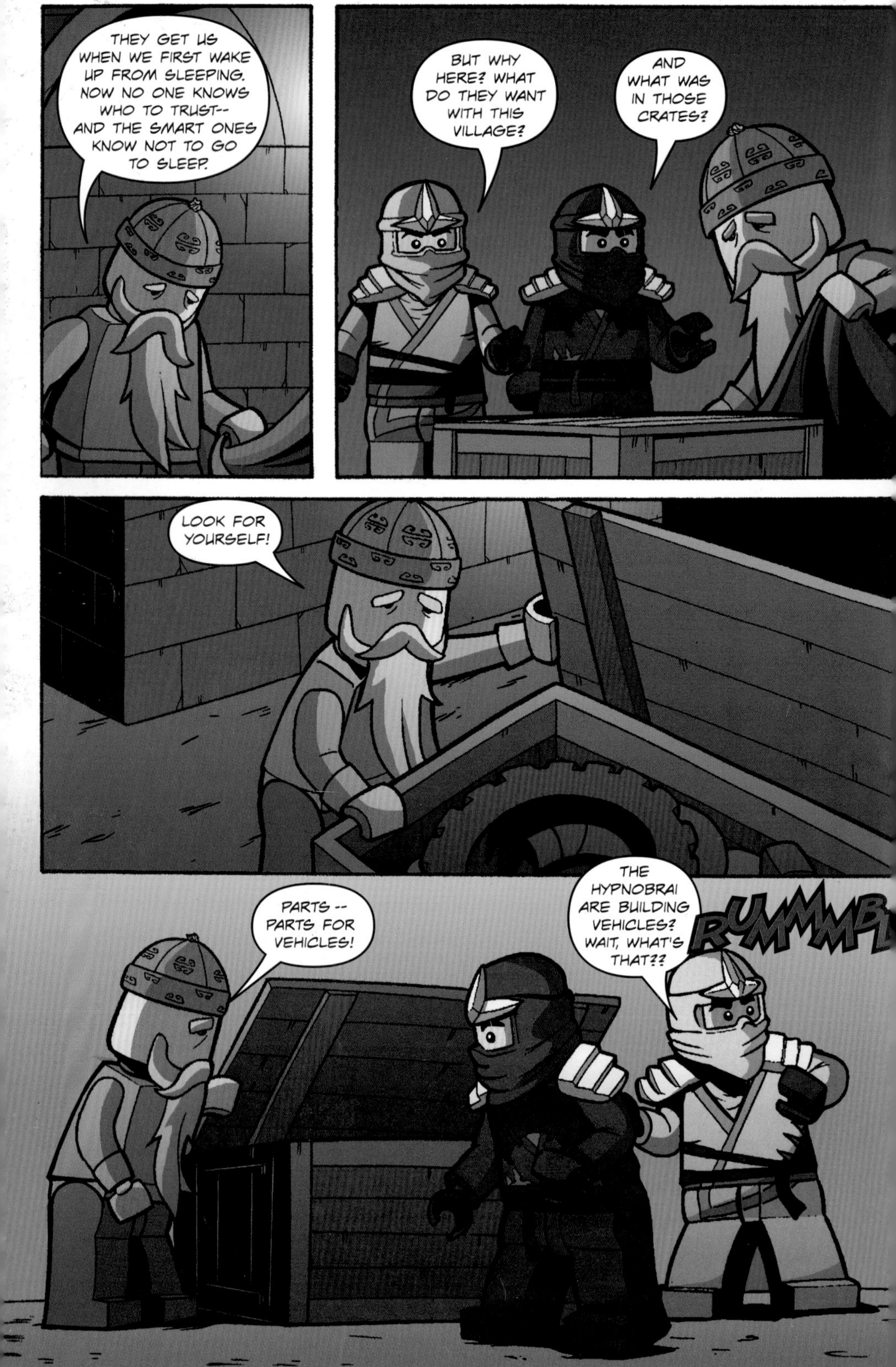
THEY GET US WHEN WE FIRST WAKE UP FROM SLEEPING. NOW NO ONE KNOWS WHO TO TRUST-- AND THE SMART ONES KNOW NOT TO GO TO SLEEP.
BUT WHY HERE? WHAT DO THEY WANT WITH THIS VILLAGE?
AND WHAT WAS IN THOSE CRATES?
LOOK FOR YOURSELF!
PARTS -- PARTS FOR VEHICLES!
THE HYPNOBRAI ARE BUILDING VEHICLES? WAIT, WHAT'S THAT??
RUMMMB

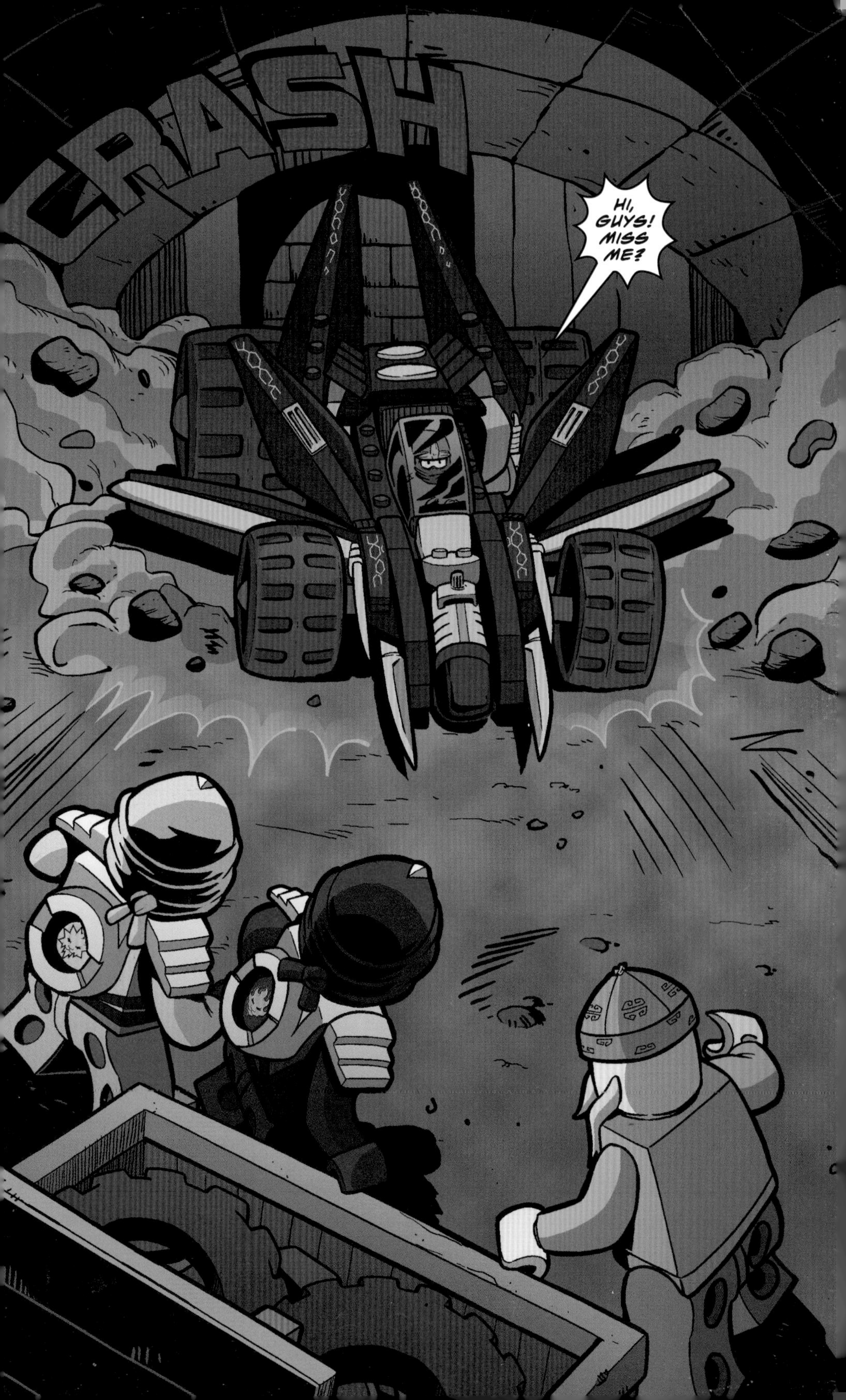
CRASH
HI, GUYS! MISS ME?

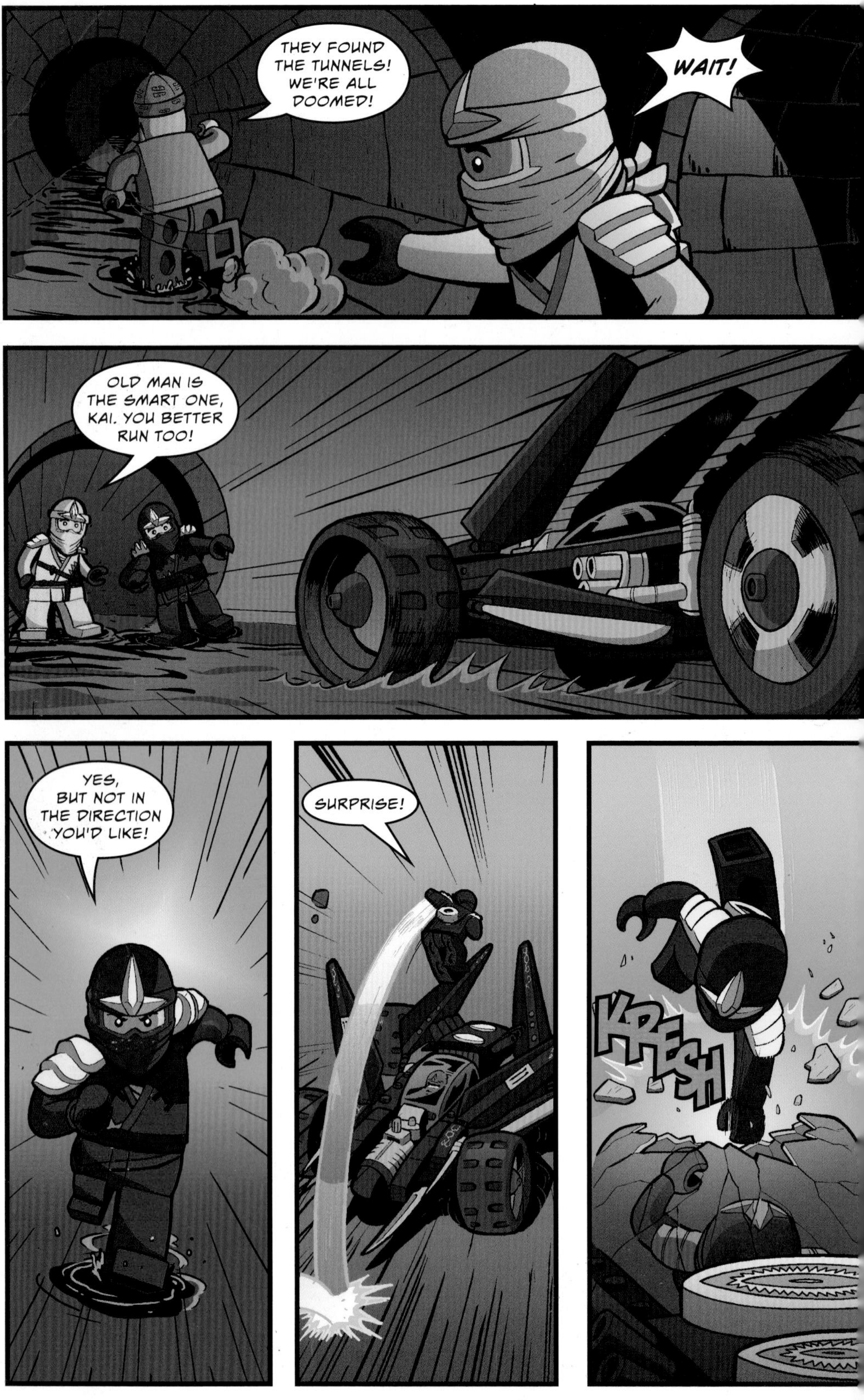
THEY FOUND THE TUNNELS! WE'RE ALL DOOMED!
WAIT!
OLD MAN IS THE SMART ONE, KAI. YOU BETTER RUN TOO!
YES, BUT NOT IN THE DIRECTION YOU'D LIKE!
SURPRISE!
KRESH

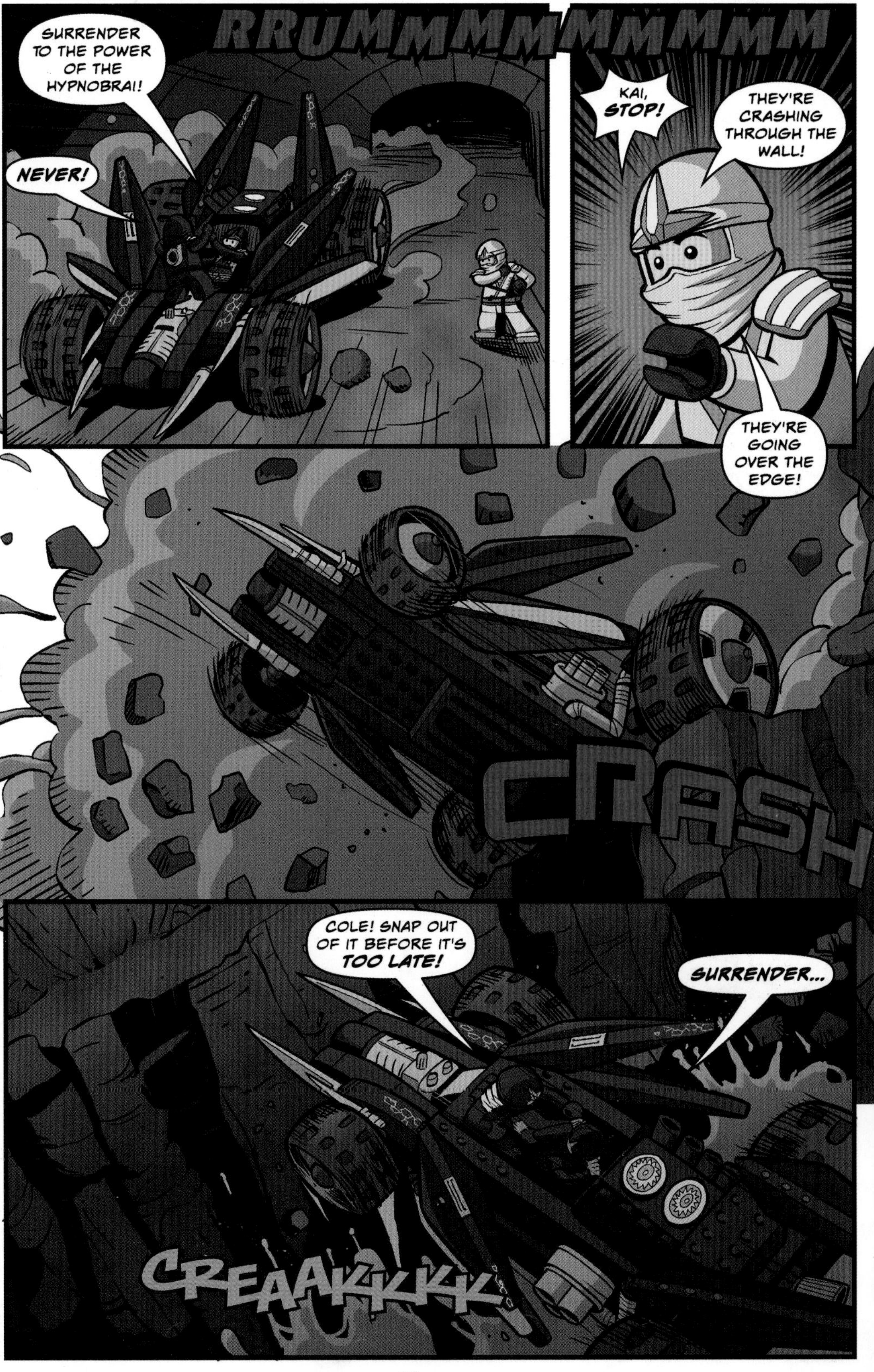

SURRENDER TO THE POWER OF THE HYPNOBRAI!
NEVER!
RRUMMMMMMMMMMM
KAI, STOP!
THEY'RE CRASHING THROUGH THE WALL!
THEY'RE GOING OVER THE EDGE!
CRASH
COLE! SNAP OUT OF IT BEFORE IT'S TOO LATE!
SURRENDER...
CREAAKKKKK

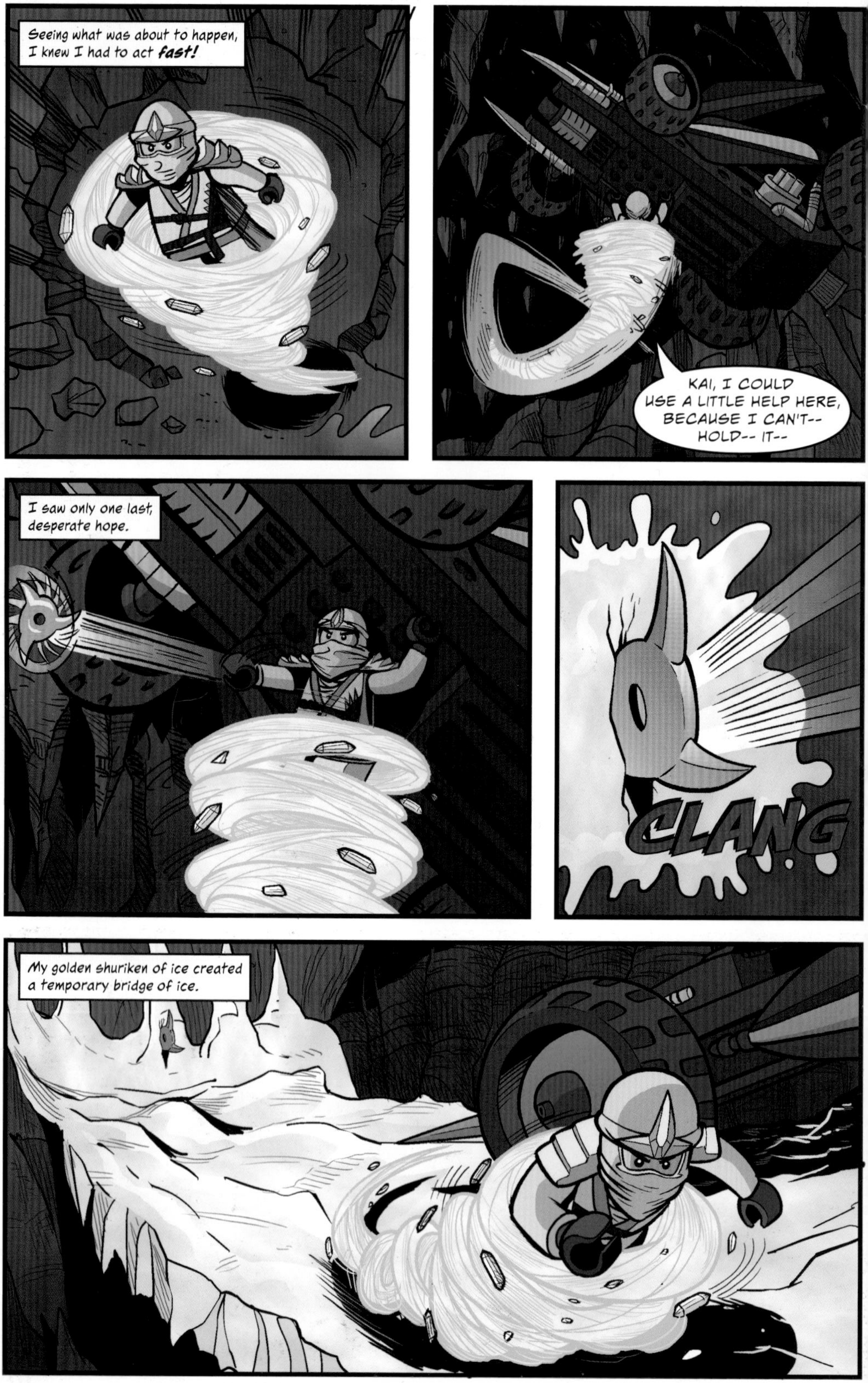
Seeing what was about to happen, I knew I had to act fast!
KAI, I COULD USE A LITTLE HELP HERE, BECAUSE I CAN'T-- HOLD-- IT--
I saw only one last, desperate hope.
CLANG
My golden shuriken of ice created a temporary bridge of ice.

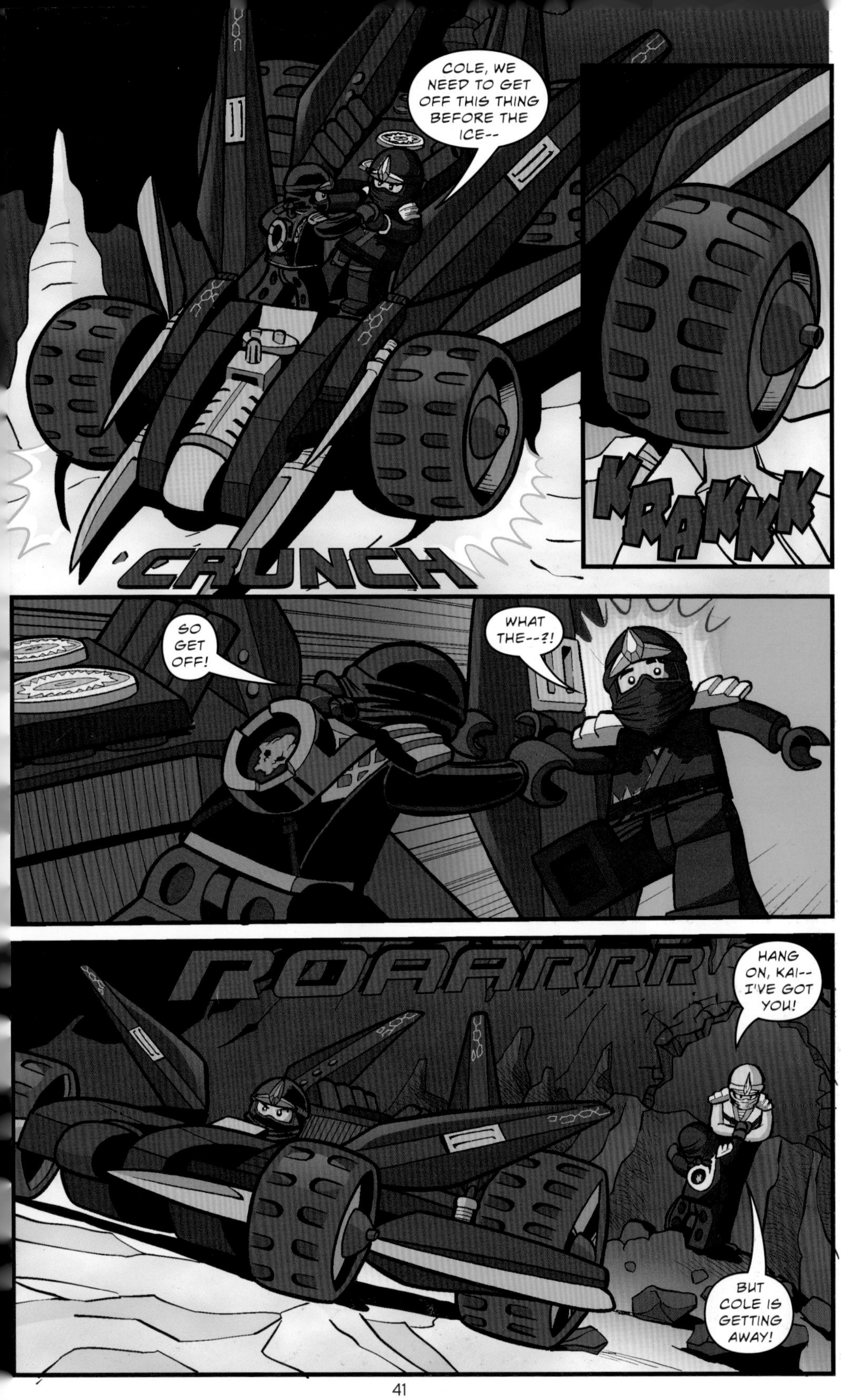
COLE, WE NEED TO GET OFF THIS THING BEFORE THE ICE--
CRUNCH
KRAKKK
SO GET OFF!
WHAT THE--?!
ROARRR
HANG ON, KAI-- I'VE GOT YOU!
BUT COLE IS GETTING AWAY!

Kai did not share his plan, insisting that we head for the warehouse the old man had mentioned. We stayed in the shadows, for obvious reasons...

Somehow, we made it to the roof of the warehouse unseen...

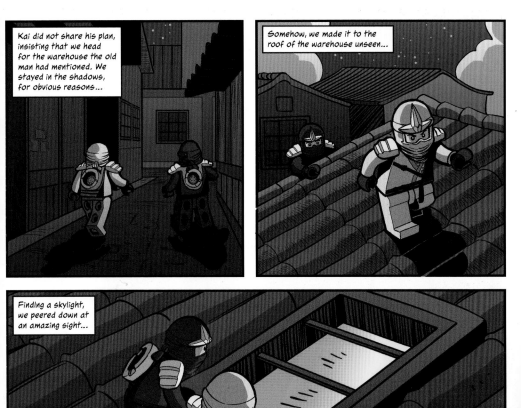

Finding a skylight, we peered down at an amazing sight...

The warehouse had been converted into a vehicle factory for the Hypnobrai!

DO WE ATTACK?

NO, TOO MANY OF THEM... EVEN FOR ME. WE WAIT!

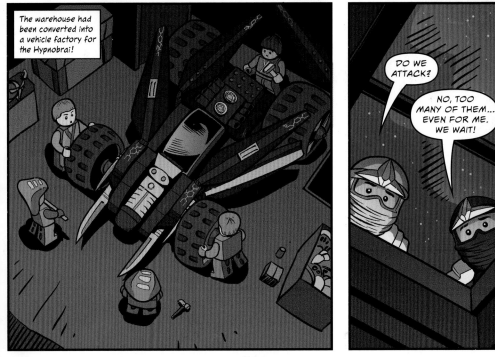

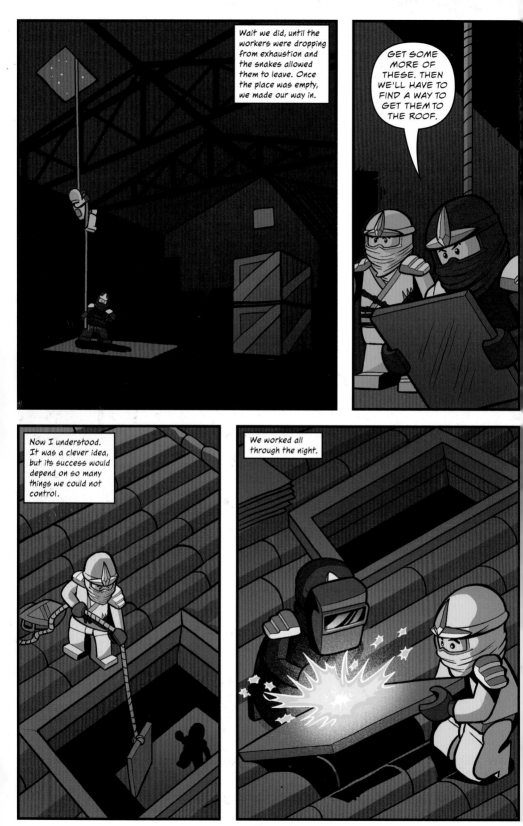

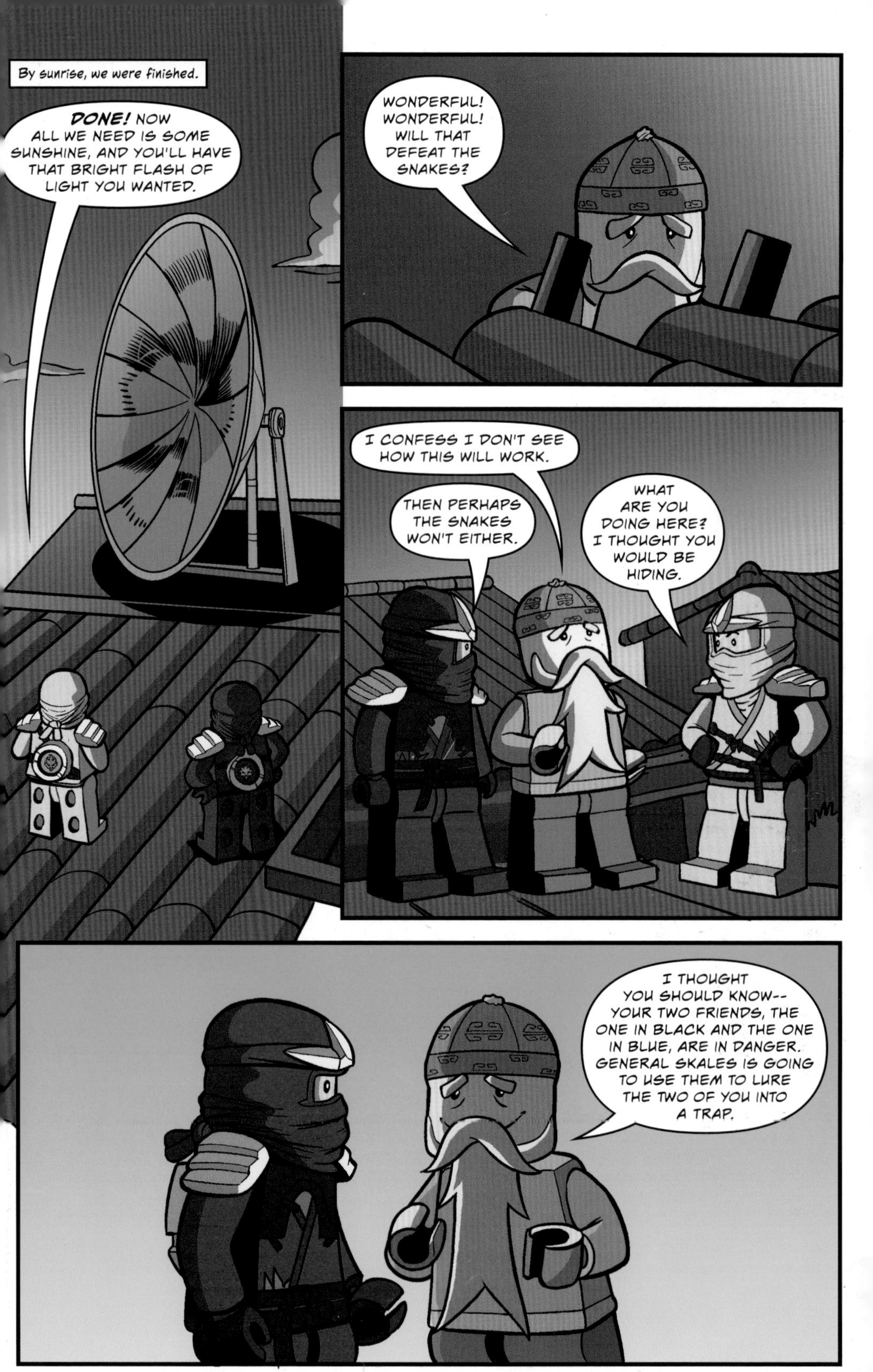
By sunrise, we were finished.
DONE! NOW ALL WE NEED IS SOME SUNSHINE, AND YOU'LL HAVE THAT BRIGHT FLASH OF LIGHT YOU WANTED.
WONDERFUL! WONDERFUL! WILL THAT DEFEAT THE SNAKES?
I CONFESS I DON'T SEE HOW THIS WILL WORK.
THEN PERHAPS THE SNAKES WON'T EITHER.
WHAT ARE YOU DOING HERE? I THOUGHT YOU WOULD BE HIDING.
I THOUGHT YOU SHOULD KNOW-- YOUR TWO FRIENDS, THE ONE IN BLACK AND THE ONE IN BLUE, ARE IN DANGER. GENERAL SKALES IS GOING TO USE THEM TO LURE THE TWO OF YOU INTO A TRAP.

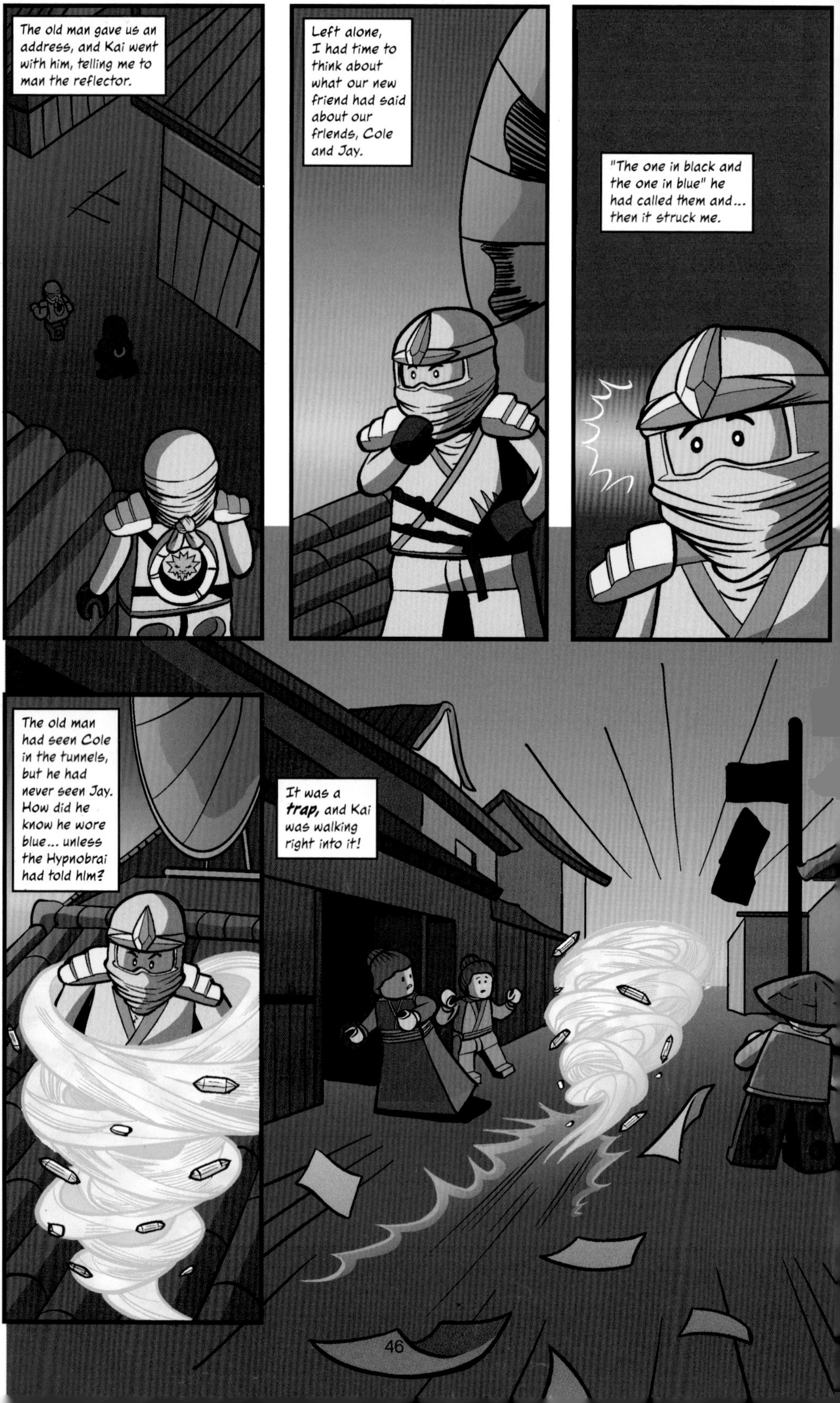

The old man gave us an address, and Kai went with him, telling me to man the reflector.
Left alone, I had time to think about what our new friend had said about our friends, Cole and Jay.
"The one in black and the one in blue" he had called them and... then it struck me.
The old man had seen Cole in the tunnels, but he had never seen Jay. How did he know he wore blue... unless the Hypnobrai had told him?
It was a *trap,* and Kai was walking right into it!

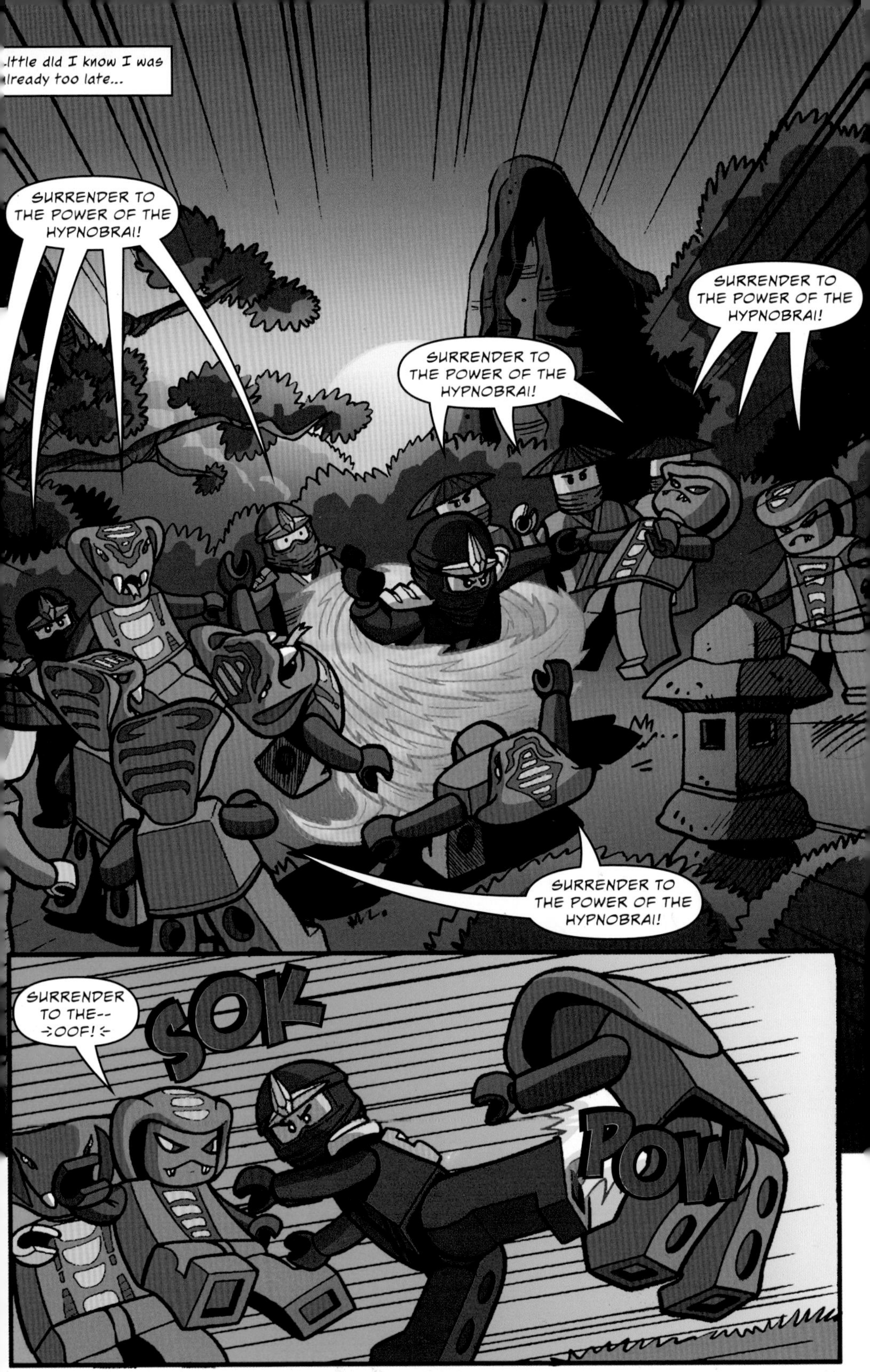
ittle did I know I was lready too late...
SURRENDER TO THE POWER OF THE HYPNOBRAI!
SURRENDER TO THE POWER OF THE HYPNOBRAI!
SURRENDER TO THE POWER OF THE HYPNOBRAI!
SURRENDER TO THE POWER OF THE HYPNOBRAI!
SURRENDER TO THE-- OOF!
SOK
POW

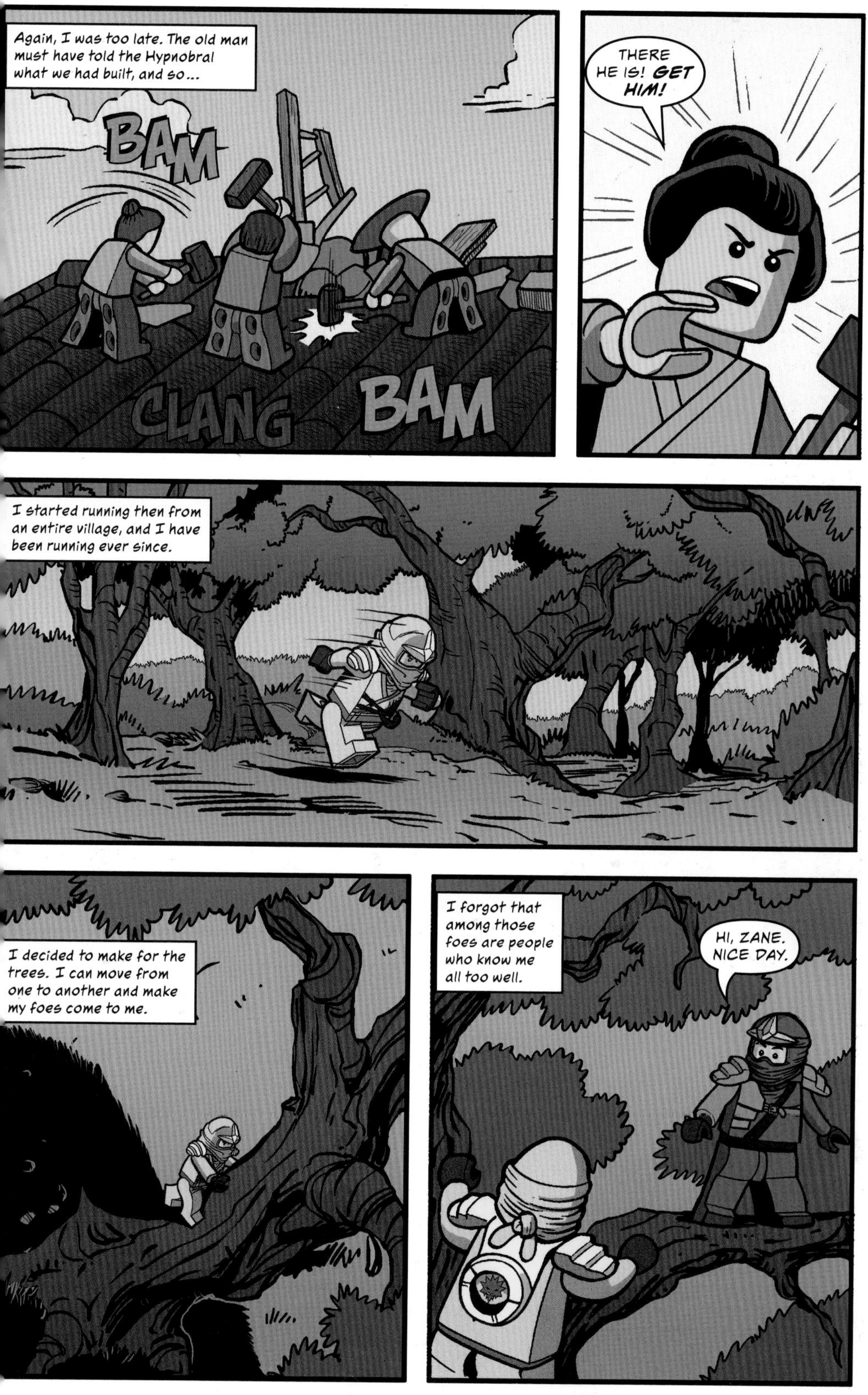
Again, I was too late. The old man must have told the Hypnobral what we had built, and so...
BAM
CLANG
BAM
THERE HE IS! GET HIM!
I started running then from an entire village, and I have been running ever since.
I decided to make for the trees. I can move from one to another and make my foes come to me.
I forgot that among those foes are people who know me all too well.
HI, ZANE. NICE DAY.

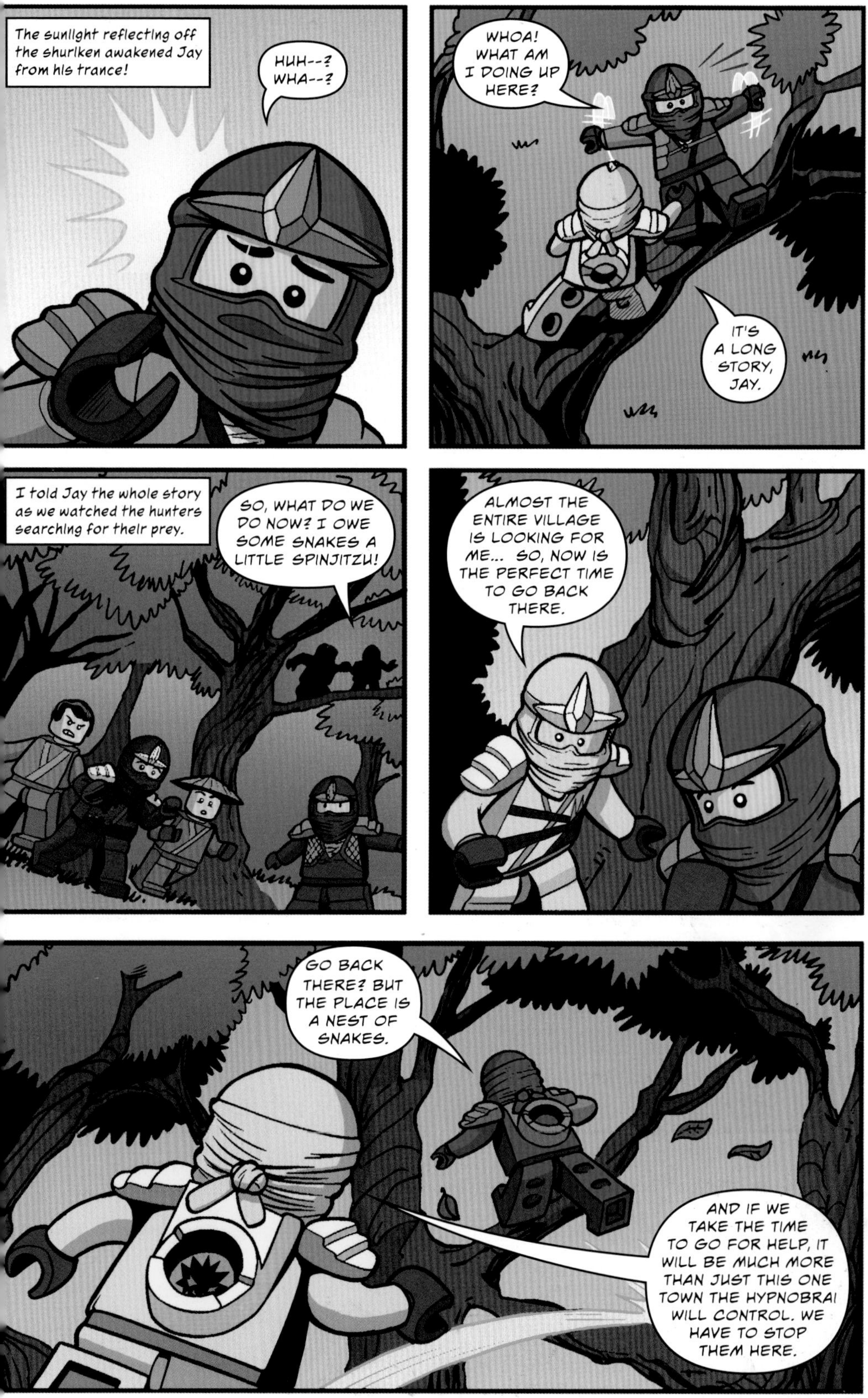
The sunlight reflecting off the shuriken awakened Jay from his trance!
HUH--? WHA--?
WHOA! WHAT AM I DOING UP HERE?
IT'S A LONG STORY, JAY.
I told Jay the whole story as we watched the hunters searching for their prey.
SO, WHAT DO WE DO NOW? I OWE SOME SNAKES A LITTLE SPINJITZU!
ALMOST THE ENTIRE VILLAGE IS LOOKING FOR ME... SO, NOW IS THE PERFECT TIME TO GO BACK THERE.
GO BACK THERE? BUT THE PLACE IS A NEST OF SNAKES.
AND IF WE TAKE THE TIME TO GO FOR HELP, IT WILL BE MUCH MORE THAN JUST THIS ONE TOWN THE HYPNOBRAI WILL CONTROL. WE HAVE TO STOP THEM HERE.

52

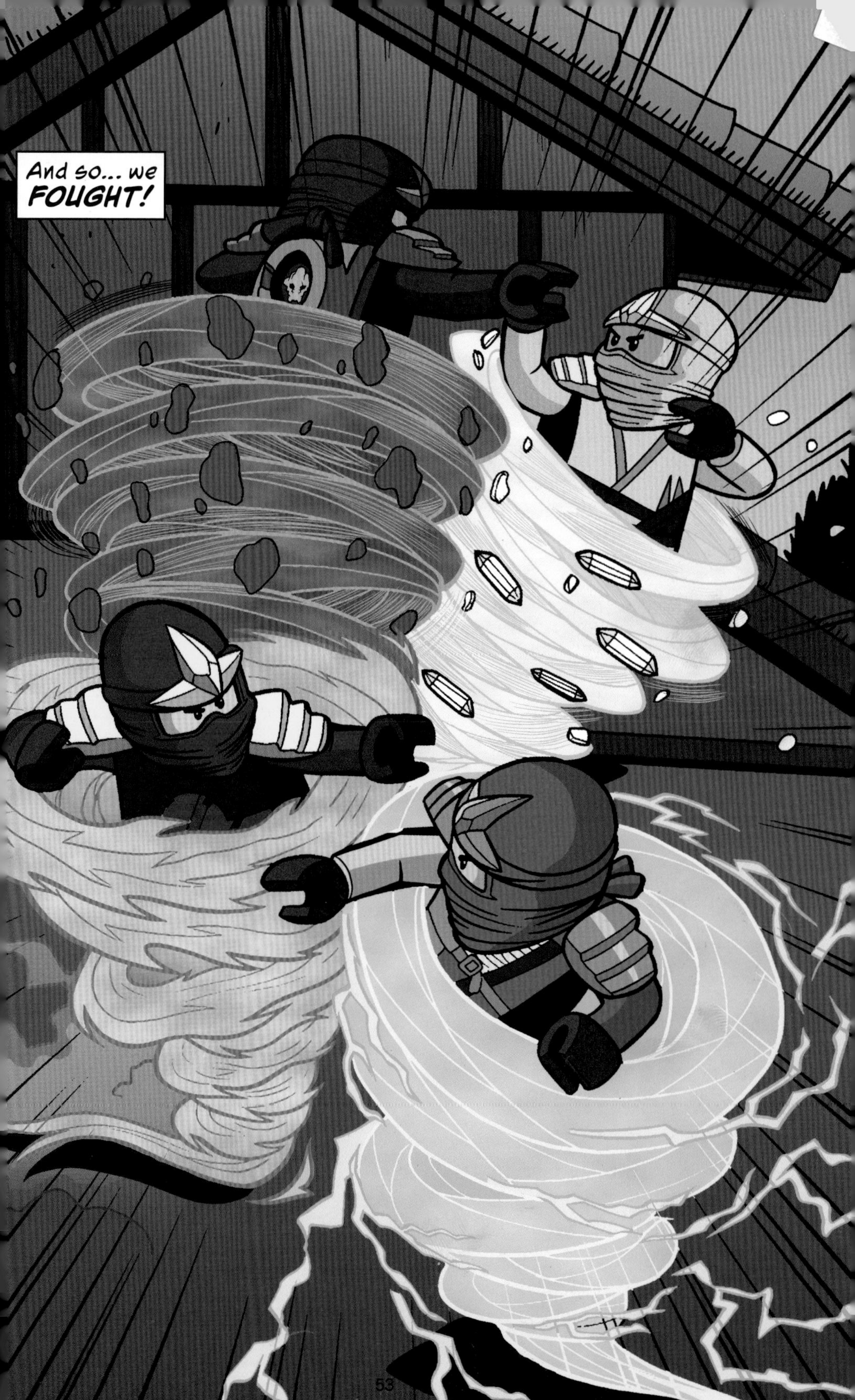
And so... we FOUGHT!

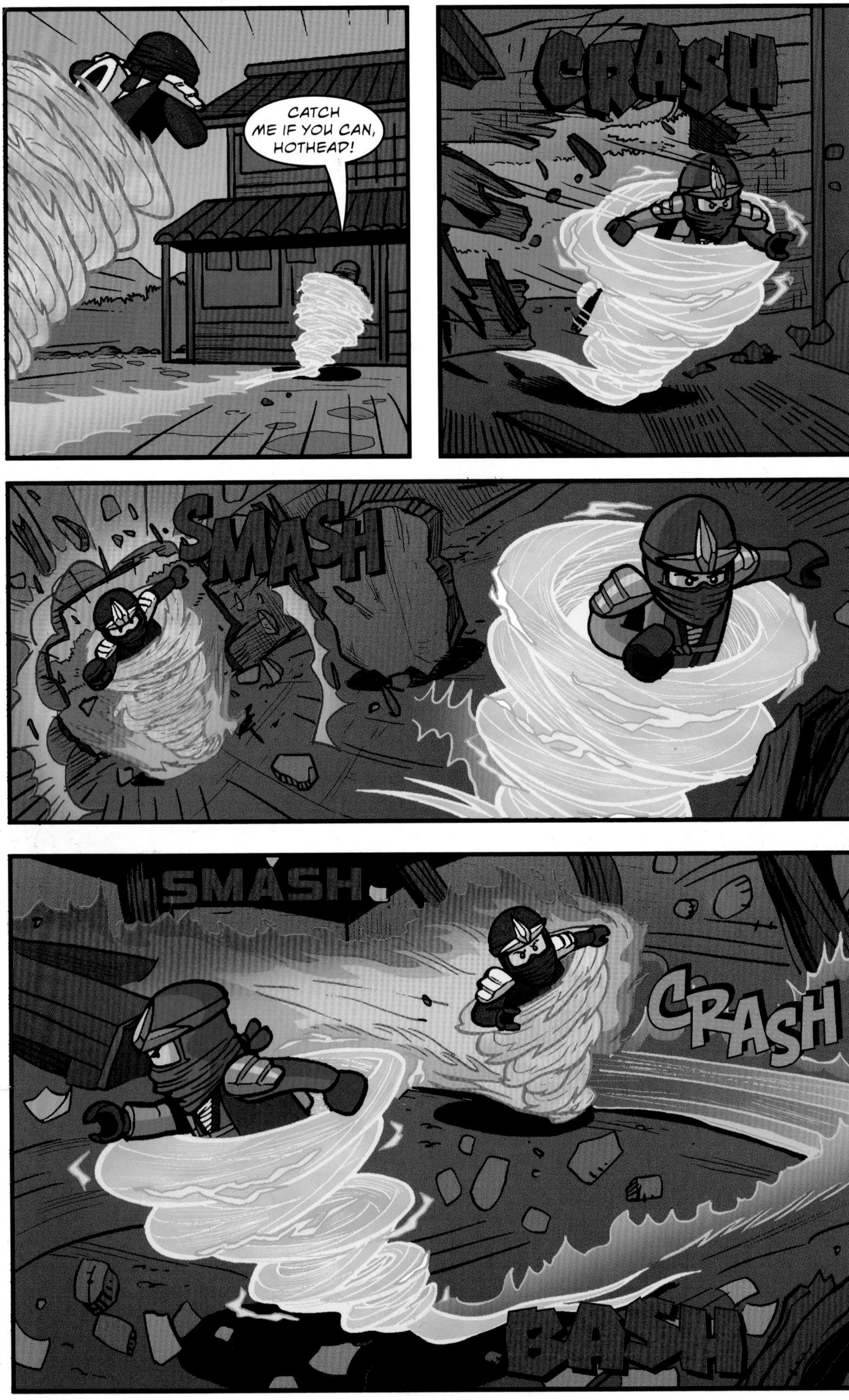
CATCH ME IF YOU CAN, HOTHEAD!
CRASH
SMASH
SMASH
CRASH
BASH

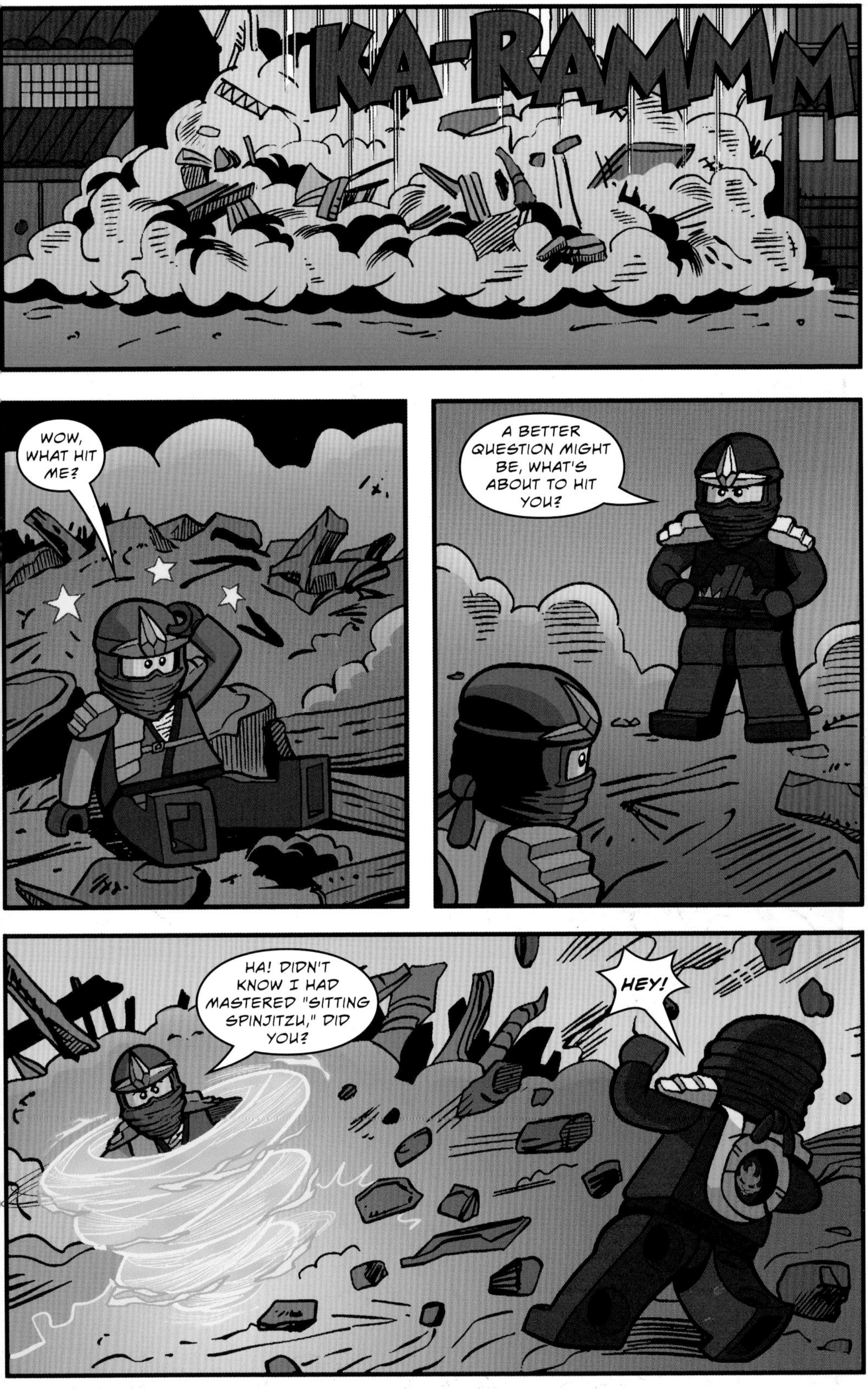
KA-RAMMM
WOW, WHAT HIT ME?
A BETTER QUESTION MIGHT BE, WHAT'S ABOUT TO HIT YOU?
HA! DIDN'T KNOW I HAD MASTERED "SITTING SPINJITZU," DID YOU?
HEY!

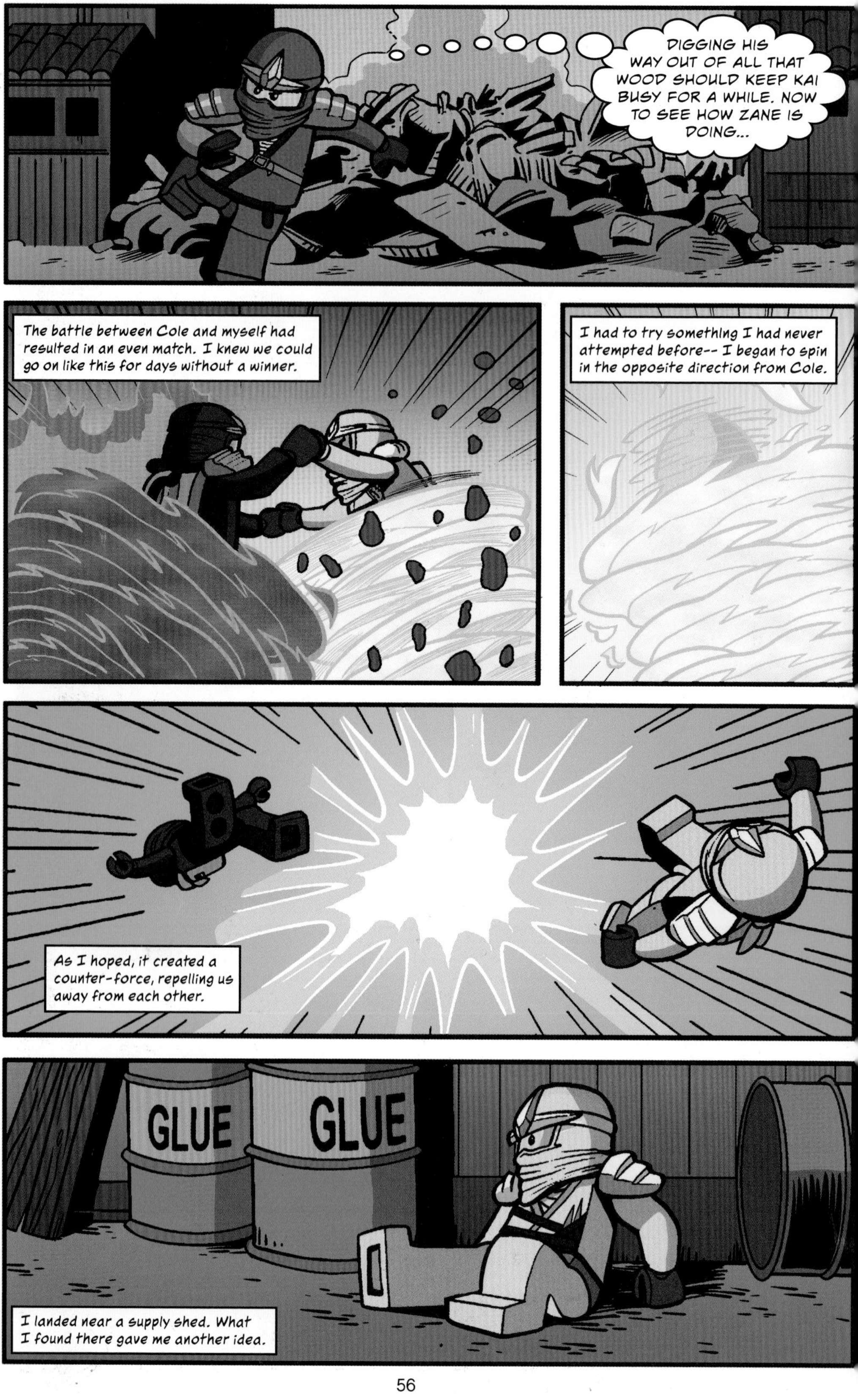
DIGGING HIS WAY OUT OF ALL THAT WOOD SHOULD KEEP KAI BUSY FOR A WHILE. NOW TO SEE HOW ZANE IS DOING...
The battle between Cole and myself had resulted in an even match. I knew we could go on like this for days without a winner.
I had to try something I had never attempted before-- I began to spin in the opposite direction from Cole.
As I hoped, it created a counter-force, repelling us away from each other.
GLUE
GLUE
I landed near a supply shed. What I found there gave me another idea.

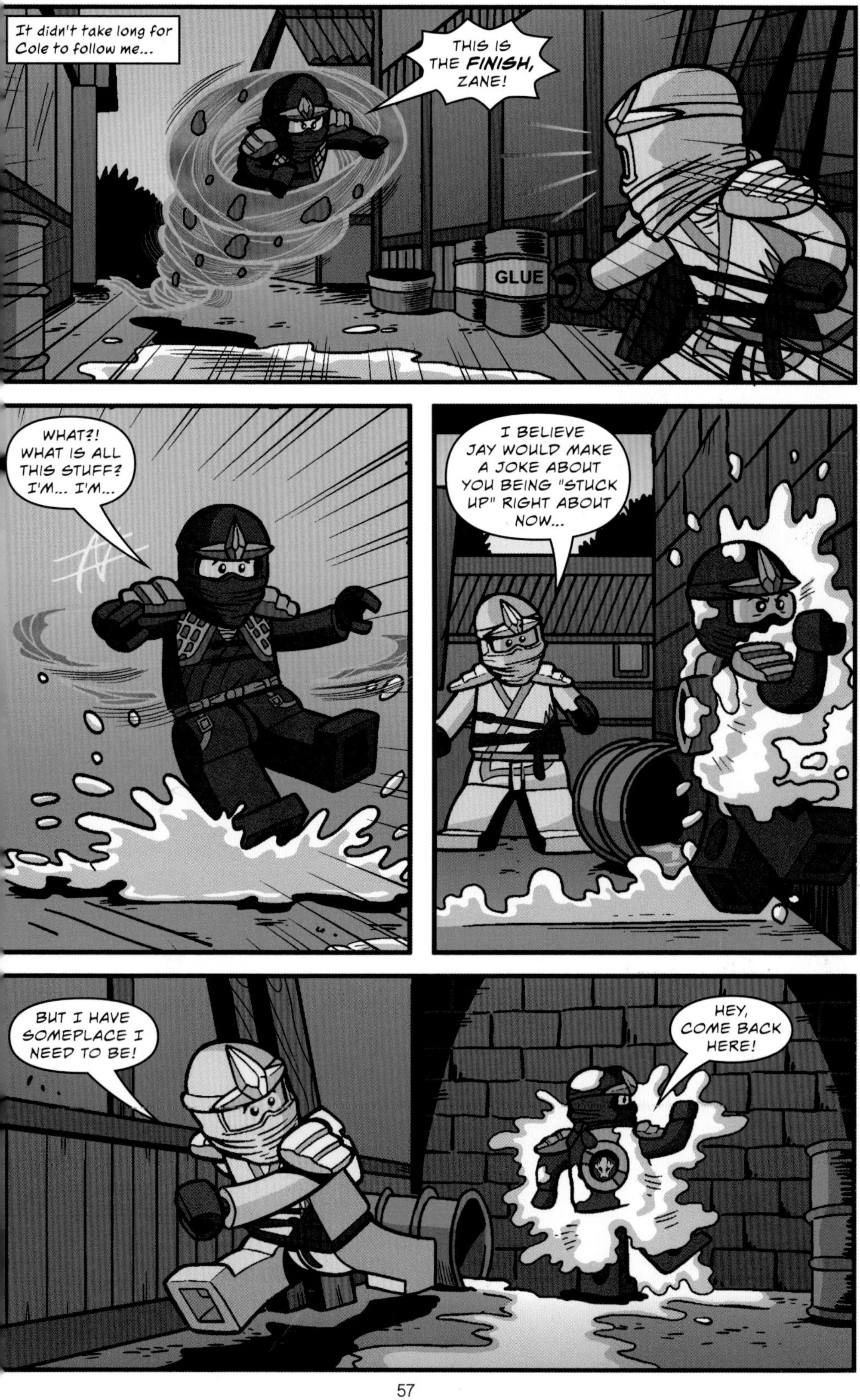
It didn't take long for Cole to follow me...
THIS IS THE FINISH, ZANE!
GLUE
WHAT?! WHAT IS ALL THIS STUFF? I'M... I'M...
I BELIEVE JAY WOULD MAKE A JOKE ABOUT YOU BEING "STUCK UP" RIGHT ABOUT NOW...
BUT I HAVE SOMEPLACE I NEED TO BE!
HEY, COME BACK HERE!

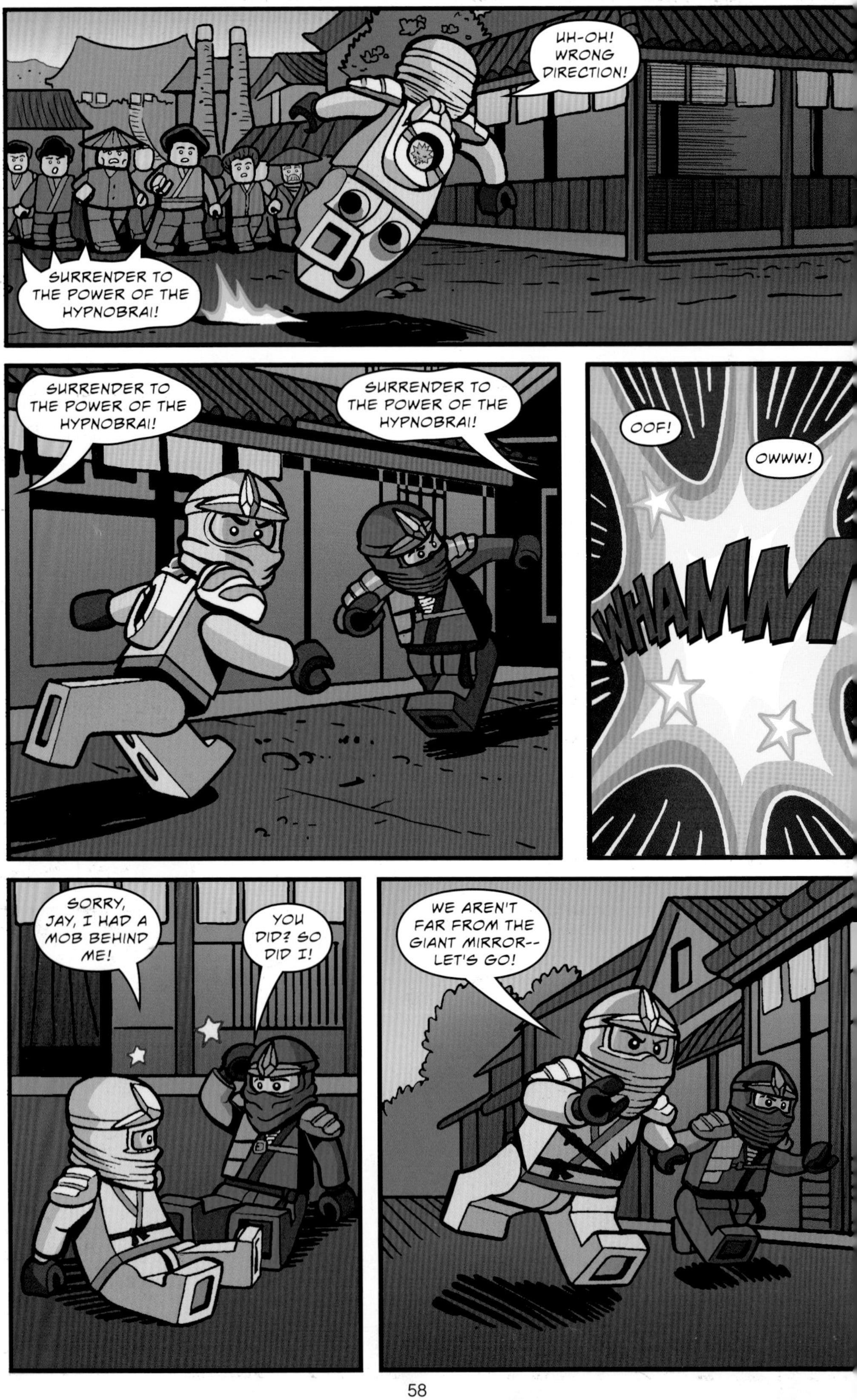
UH-OH! WRONG DIRECTION!
SURRENDER TO THE POWER OF THE HYPNOBRAI!
SURRENDER TO THE POWER OF THE HYPNOBRAI!
SURRENDER TO THE POWER OF THE HYPNOBRAI!
OOF!
OWWW!
WHAMM
SORRY, JAY, I HAD A MOB BEHIND ME!
YOU DID? SO DID I!
WE AREN'T FAR FROM THE GIANT MIRROR-- LET'S GO!

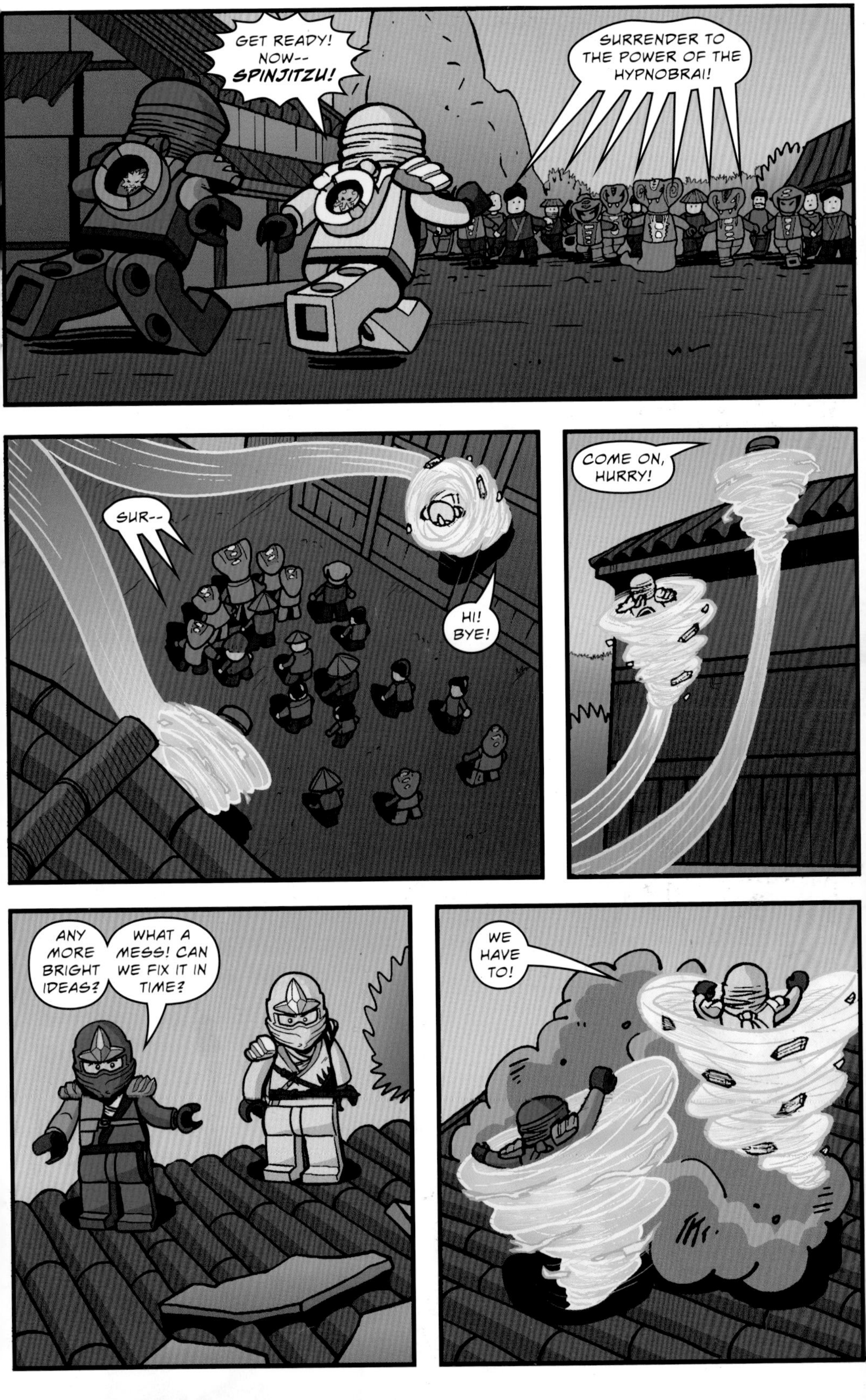
GET READY! NOW-- SPINJITZU!
SURRENDER TO THE POWER OF THE HYPNOBRAI!
SUR--
HI! BYE!
COME ON, HURRY!
ANY MORE BRIGHT IDEAS?
WHAT A MESS! CAN WE FIX IT IN TIME?
WE HAVE TO!

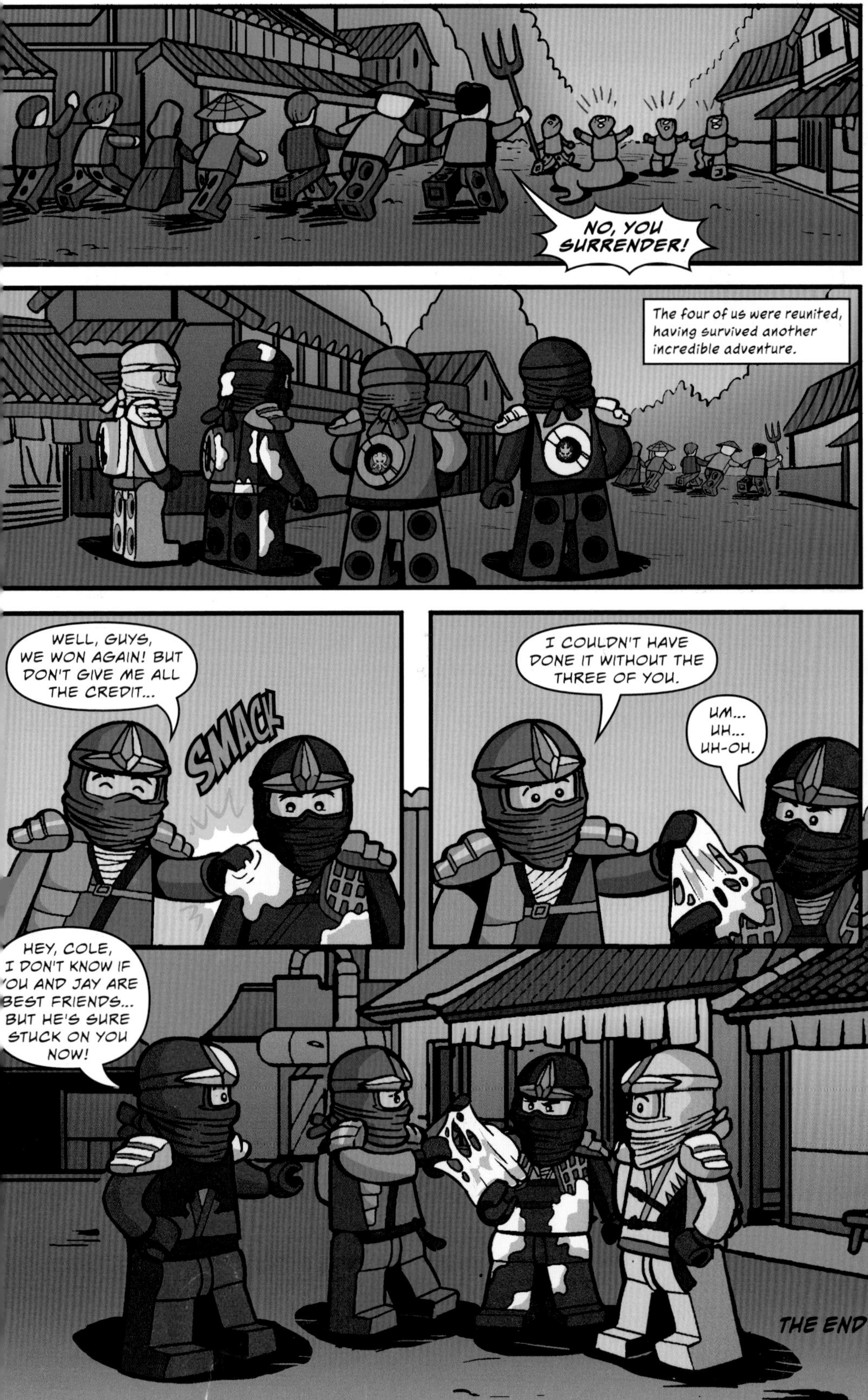
NO, YOU SURRENDER!
The four of us were reunited, having survived another incredible adventure.
WELL, GUYS, WE WON AGAIN! BUT DON'T GIVE ME ALL THE CREDIT...
SMACK
I COULDN'T HAVE DONE IT WITHOUT THE THREE OF YOU.
UM... UH... UH-OH.
HEY, COLE, I DON'T KNOW IF OU AND JAY ARE BEST FRIENDS... BUT HE'S SURE STUCK ON YOU NOW!
THE END

SNEAK PEEK

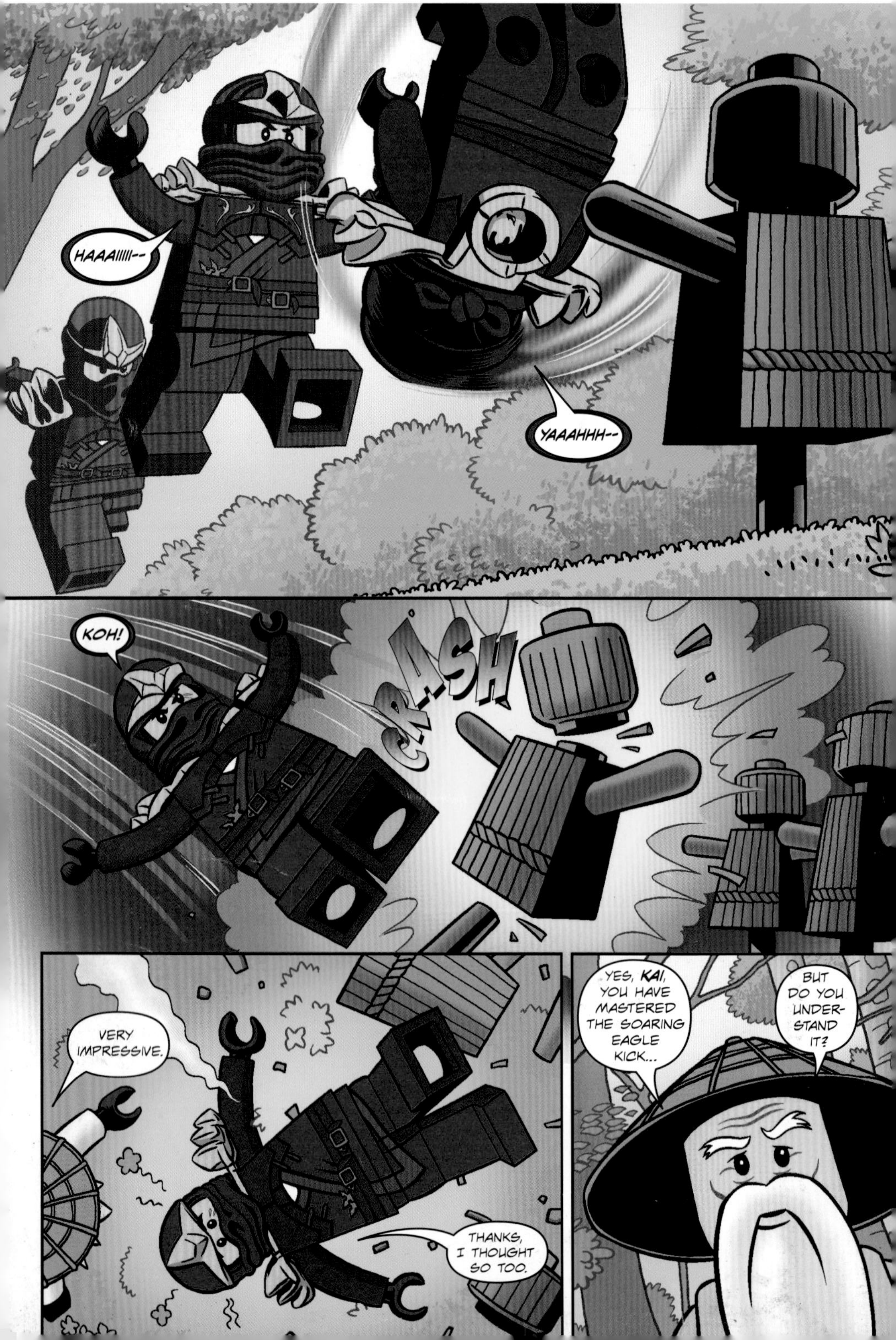
HAAAIIIII--
YAAAHHH--
KOH!
CRASH
VERY IMPRESSIVE.
THANKS, I THOUGHT SO TOO.
YES, KAI, YOU HAVE MASTERED THE SOARING EAGLE KICK...
BUT DO YOU UNDER-STAND IT?

VOLUME 4

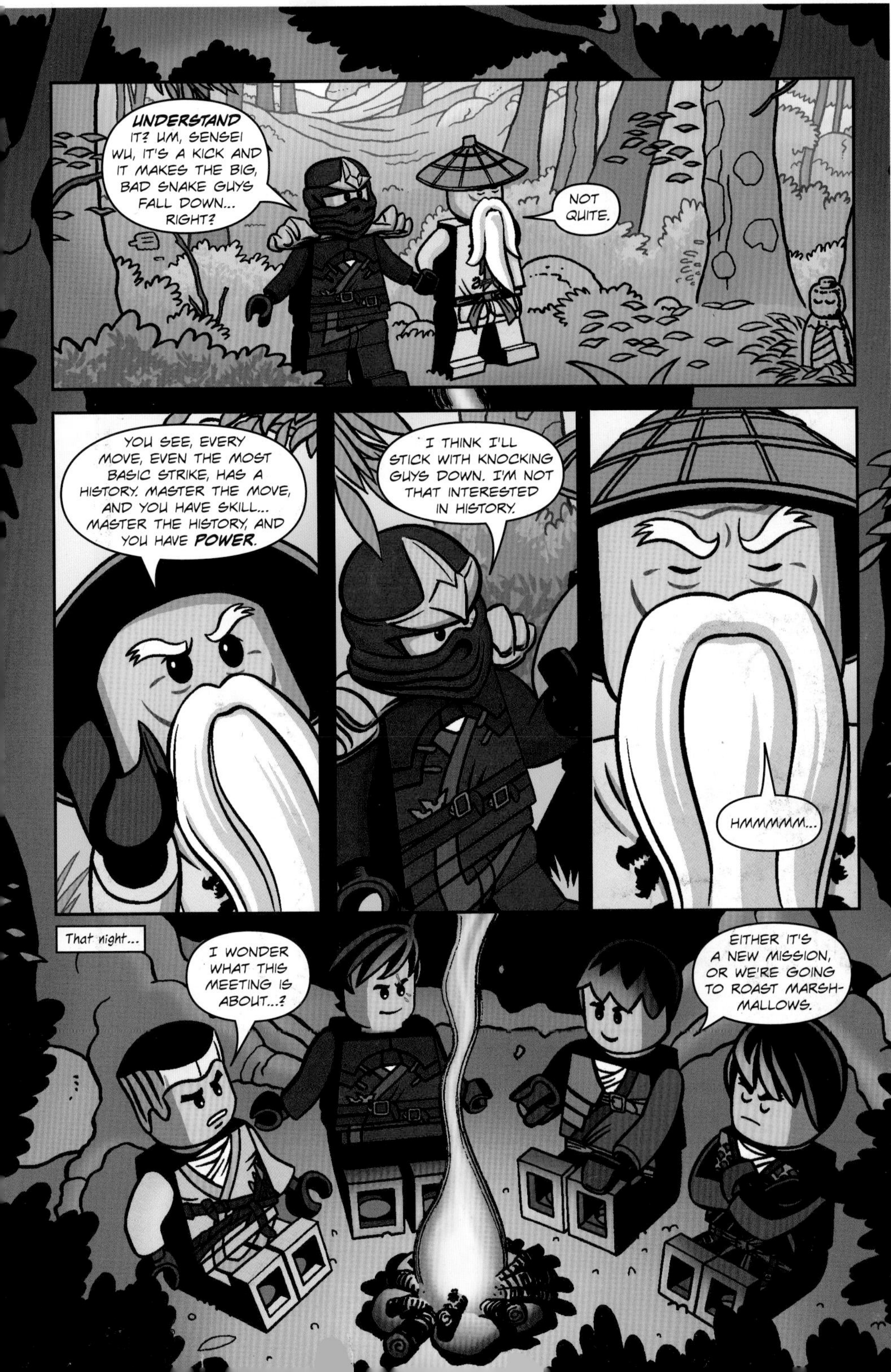
UNDERSTAND IT? UM, SENSEI WU, IT'S A KICK AND IT MAKES THE BIG, BAD SNAKE GUYS FALL DOWN... RIGHT?
NOT QUITE.
YOU SEE, EVERY MOVE, EVEN THE MOST BASIC STRIKE, HAS A HISTORY. MASTER THE MOVE, AND YOU HAVE SKILL... MASTER THE HISTORY, AND YOU HAVE POWER.
I THINK I'LL STICK WITH KNOCKING GUYS DOWN. I'M NOT THAT INTERESTED IN HISTORY.
HMMMMM...
That night...
I WONDER WHAT THIS MEETING IS ABOUT...?
EITHER IT'S A NEW MISSION, OR WE'RE GOING TO ROAST MARSH-MALLOWS.